RHYMING HISTORY

The Story of England in Verse

RHYMING HISTORY
The Story of England in Verse

by Colin Wakefield

Illustrations by John Partridge

VOLUME ONE: 55BC – 1485

The Romans to
The Wars of the Roses

DHP
Double Honours Publications

RHYMING HISTORY
The Story of England in Verse

VOLUME ONE: 55BC – 1485
The Romans to the Wars of the Roses

First published in 2011 by Double Honours Publications.

ISBN 978-0-9570120-0-4

Double Honours Publications

Email: info@rhyminghistory.co.uk
Website: www.rhyminghistory.co.uk

Printed by Good News Digital Books.

AUTHOR'S NOTE

This is Volume One of a longer *Rhyming History* of mine (still in the writing), which will eventually stretch from Julius Caesar's invasion of Britain in 55BC to the present day.

Volume Two (The Tudors) will appear in 2012, with subsequent volumes published annually. An audio CD of excerpts will be produced simultaneously with each new volume. The CD of Volume One is available for sale through the website.

I had no great success with history at school, so set about educating myself in later life. These books of verse are directed at people like me who want to learn about our history, but in not too solemn a way. I hope they will also appeal to a wider audience, students and historians, and those who simply enjoy reading poetry.

John Partridge has provided witty and entertaining illustrations to accompany the text, for which I am most grateful.

Special thanks to Jonathan Dowie for preparation of the text, Chris Moss for help with the cover, Malcolm Oxley for expert advice, and Michael Callahan for invaluable support.

Please visit our website for updates on future volumes of the *History*, and for news of live performances of the verse.

www.rhyminghistory.co.uk

Colin Wakefield – September 2011

THE ROMANS

Julius Caesar, in 55 BC,   **55 BC**
Gaul having been conquered (and no slouch he),
Decided, like many a tyrant before,
That Gaul was not enough. He wanted more.
Many there were who thought he was barmy,
Yet he set sail (with his Roman army)
For the fabled shores of Britain, where there dwelt
A tribe renowned for warlike deeds, the Celt:
Heroic hunter-gatherers, a breed
Skilled in the art of bronze, and fond of mead.

Only a short day-trip, you understand,
A little *recce* (that was all he planned),
With a small force, nothing fancy or grand.
He made a quick survey, ten miles inland,
Then turned round. But Caesar liked what he saw.
The next year he was back, for all-out war.   **54 BC**

Rhyming History

This time the Romans were ready for battle
And slaughtered the Celts like so many cattle.
Their legions: well-ordered, disciplined, first rate;
The Celts in their chariots, all out of date.
Despite the heroic resistance of some,
The Age of the Roman had truly begun.

Or had it? Caesar suffered troubles in Gaul.
He and his successors had no time at all
For these rebellious Celts across the sea.
British gold (and slaves) were of poor quality,
And payment of tribute hard to guarantee.
Some Romans began tacitly to agree
With Caesar's generals. They'd been largely right:
The Celtic campaigns were hardly worth the fight.

Almost a century passed before the occasion
Of the next, more significant, Roman invasion.
But Caesar left his mark: a growth in trade –
In skins, in precious metals, pearls and jade,
Exchange of ideas, how things were made.

Memories of conquest began to fade.
Britain forgot Rome, but not *vice versa.*
Julius Caesar was the precursor
Of Emperor Claudius. In 43 –   **AD 43**
In the Year of our Lord, so now it's 'AD' –
Claudius succeeded (unexpectedly)
His nephew, Caligula. Take it from me,
Caligula was weak and quite unable
To run a bath-house, let alone… "Unstable"
Is the word that I'd use. Assassination
Was too good for him. But his fascination
With all things British made him draw up a plan
For conquest, in detail to the very last man –
Which he called off the morning before it began.

The Romans to the Wars of the Roses

Claudius was a funny sort of chap.
Folk thought he'd suffered some kind of mishap
At birth. Bookish and reserved, he stuttered –
And when he did speak, he simply spluttered.
Most of his life he'd been largely ignored,
But now he proved a wizard with the sword.
Sorry, that's not quite true. He was rotten
At fighting himself, but soon forgotten
Were his faults and foibles. He seized his chance,
Led his triumphant forces up through France
(That's Gaul to you), his troops all cock-a-hoop,
And subdued the British in one fell swoop.

With 40,000 men – hardly surprising.
After resistance (and the odd uprising),
The Brits capitulated. Eleven Kings
Declared themselves Claudius's underlings.
The Emperor, thrilled with these developments,
Rode in pomp to Colchester (with elephants).

The Roman Empire grew to this extent:
Due west to the Severn, north to the Trent.
Beyond these borders, in tougher terrain,
The Romans would suffer, time and again,
From raids and rebellions, pillage and plots,
By those wild marauders, the Picts and the Scots.

That's the story for the next three hundred years,
Give or take. Empires, they always end in tears.
Spectacular was Queen Boudicca's revolt.
The Romans weren't expecting her assault.
In 60 (or 61) she united   **AD 60**
A taskforce of Brits and stormed, uninvited,
Through London and Colchester. Both she laid waste,
Which the Romans considered in pretty poor taste.

3

In due course of time the revolt was suppressed,
And Boudicca cruelly tortured (you guessed).

Soon the invader began to feel at home,
Aping the manners of Imperial Rome.
Aquae Sulis was established as a Bath,
Where the ruling classes went to have a laugh.
Five important cities sprang up: Colchester,
Verulamium, Lincoln, York and Gloucester.
Villas appeared in the Italian style,
With London famed in matters mercantile;
And those Roman roads: Watling Street, the Fosse Way –
Straight as a die, and with us to this day.

At the latest, by AD 84,   **AD 84**
The Empire stretched to Scotland's northern shore.
But this availed the Romans not a jot,
With much time wasted on the moody Scot.
Hadrian, in 122, said, "Hang it all!   **122**
"I've had enough of this. I'll build a wall" –
Which, true to his word, he did. He drew a line
From Solway in the west across to the Tyne,

And that's where he built it. Far-sighted and wise,
He called it "Hadrian's Wall" – surprise, surprise.

This kept out the troublesome Scots for a while,
Yet they were the final victors, by a mile.
Whenever the Romans were down in the mouth,
The Scots (and the Picts) would go pillaging south.
A similar pattern emerged in the west:
If the Celts could cause trouble, they'd do their best.

We can now move on a century or two.
When the going got tough, what did they do
(The Romans, I mean)? Under pressure in Gaul,
They tended to take their eye off the ball.
The Franks and the Saxons, in 367, **367**
Stormed through Gaul. This was manna from Heaven
For the Picts and Scots, who banded together
And charged into Britain, hell-for-leather,
To rout the dispirited Romans. In short,
After four hundred years, the Empire was caught
(Excuse the expression) with its toga down.
Scarcely a fortress, a villa or town
Survived the onslaught. To add to the mess,
Saxon pirates were enjoying success
In raids on Britain's unfortified shore.
The Empire faced ruin as never before.

Emperor Valentinian, however,
Had other ideas. It was now or never.
He despatched Theodosius, with a force,
To defeat the Barbarians; which, of course –
With a Roman commander's courage and skill –
He did, in most notable fashion, until
The enemy was routed, London relieved,
Order restored, and a just peace achieved.

Even the Saxons suffered losses at sea.
They were holding their fire, if you ask me,

Till the Romans finally lost the plot,
Which they would in due course, like it or not.

After Emperor Theodosius died   **395**
(Theodosius's grandson – glorified
As 'the Great': quite right, too), it can't be denied
That the Romans were set on a downward slide.
Constantine's army was under attack
In Spain, and effectively turned its back
On Britain, itself in need of support.
The Brits were feeling decidedly fraught.
Things came to a head. The army rebelled,
And Constantine's government was expelled.

The Romanised Britons were now on their own,   **409**
To face Saxon and Celt, Pict and Scot, alone.

THE ANGLO-SAXONS

Centuries passed, shrouded in mystery.
Bede's great *Ecclesiastical History* –
Hundreds of years on, in 731,
A fine work of scholarship, second to none –
Is one of the few records to survive.
But Bede, remember, wasn't writing 'live':
He learnt from sources, sixth- or seventh-hand,
How the first 'English' settled in the land.
Saxons (from Saxony), Angles and Jutes
Set sail in their thousands to put down roots –
Landing at first on the lowlands of Kent,
Sowing destruction wherever they went.

Bede's Germanic ancestors were rough,
Warlike, ruthless, battle-scarred and tough –
Storming through the country with fire and sword,
A wild, undisciplined, unruly horde.
Audacious deeds bound brigands together,
Loyalty to lord, whatever the weather.

Settlers chanted sea-faring sagas,
Celebrating feats of famous forefathers:
Savage, romantic, people of passion –
Hacking to death, according to fashion.

At Mons Badonicus, Gildas asserts,
In the year 500 the edge reverts   **500**
To the British. With a fine new leader
(King Arthur? Perhaps…), he tells the reader,
They won a great victory. Fifty years
Of peace, he claims, followed. This, though, appears
A wild overstatement. By Gildas's time,
The British revival was well past its prime.

By the mid-sixth century, all agree
That Britain (or 'England') was a 'Heptarchy' –
Seven kingdoms. Wessex, Mercia, Kent
And East Anglia (to a lesser extent)
Were the major players, with (in the north)
Northumbria, up to the Firth of Forth.
Don't be deceived. There was no unity,
No sense of 'national community'.
You've heard of the Dark Ages. These were they,
Tribal warfare the order of the day.
Civilisation went badly astray.
In Gildas's words: "Wicked tyrants held sway."

Christianity

As Britons fled north and west (or to France),
Christianity struggled to stand a chance.
The Anglo-Saxons worshipped pagan gods,
And yet the Church held on, against the odds.
The Celts in Wales helped religion survive,
Keeping the flame of Christianity alive.

Celtic Christianity was just one strand
Of a religious revival. On the one hand

Came Columba from Ireland, in the west,
To Scotland, where he did his level best
To convert the heathens. In 563   **563**
He established, highly successfully,
On the Isle of Iona, his mission.
Hard graft, and many an expedition
By his missionary monks, converted
Hordes of heathen Picts. Sure, some reverted
To type, as you'd expect. I'd say, though, on the whole,
That British Christianity was on a roll.

On the other hand there landed in Kent,
In 597, Augustine. He'd been sent   **597**
By Pope Gregory the Great (so they say)
To turn 'Angles' into 'Angels' – well, hey,
It's a good story, but I'm telling you
That, whether or not the legend is true,
Augustine (later a Saint) succeeded,
And proved exactly what England needed.

He founded the see of Canterbury,
The seat of Roman Christianity
In these islands. King Ethelbert of Kent
Was converted and, wherever he went,
Augustine laboured so that men should know
The teachings of Christ. But progress was slow.
London stayed stubbornly pagan. Success
For many decades rested, more or less,
On the whim of individual Kings,
Like Penda of Mercia, whose leanings
Remained strongly pro-Tiw, Woden and Thor
(Norse pagan gods). Mercia was at war
With neighbouring Northumbria. Their King
(Converted in 627), Edwin,   **627**
Was slain by Penda ('Christian hater')
In 632, a mere five years later.   **632**

Religion, though, now had a foothold.
Edwin's Christian successor, Oswald,
Determined to keep the Gospel alive.
He sent to Iona, in 635, **635**
To invite one Aidan over as preacher,
Bishop, missionary and teacher,
To spread the word of God throughout the land
In language simple folk would understand.

Writing nearly a century later,
Bede (no contemporary spectator)
Nevertheless contends, page after page,
That these early years were the golden age
Of ecclesiastical history.
It remains something of a mystery
How Aidan did it. Monasteries galore,
Like Lindisfarne, and churches by the score
He built. His missionary monks, with zeal,
Went out on foot like Aidan, their appeal
(According to Bede) a humble authority,
Meeting passers-by on terms of equality.

Aidan's influence spread further afield,
Into Mercia. Penda didn't yield,
Yet when his own son went and got baptized,
Penda was neither upset nor surprised.

This didn't herald peace. Far from it. No –
Penda slew Oswald, ever his sworn foe,
At Oswestry, in 642. Oswy,   **642**
True champion of Christianity
(Oswald's brother and successor), in turn
Killed Penda, leading to a swift return
Of Church influence, not just in the north,
But throughout the southern kingdoms. Henceforth,
I can report, without fear of contradiction,
Most of England was basically Christian.

Ominous storms were brewing, however.
Roman and Celtic Christians never
(And I repeat, never) saw eye to eye –
Given their common cause, one wonders why.
Entrenched for centuries in the Welsh hills,
The Celts still blamed the Saxons for their ills.
Welsh Christians even fought with Penda –
And he a die-hard pagan, remember –
Against King Edwin, and Oswald the Bold.

Never inclined to do as they were told,
The Celts (Irish and Welsh) would celebrate
Easter on a strictly different date
From that chosen by the Romans. This meant
That Oswy's wife (Roman: brought up in Kent)
Could conceivably be observing Lent
While Oswy (Irish-Celtic) was hell-bent
On celebrating Easter. This issue,
Fraught and vexed, was resolved (with some to-do)
When Oswy, on his wife's advice, forebore,
At the Synod of Whitby (664),   **664**

To back the Celts. Game, set and match to Rome.
The Celts, some in high dudgeon, trooped off home,
Back to Iona; and, till Henry's day
(The Eighth, that is), the Roman Church held sway.

I've dwelt at length (and won't apologise)
On the growth of religion; the great prize:
Civilization, the gift of learning.
The Church encouraged the most discerning
Of its disciples in the basic arts
Of reading and writing, reaching the parts
That pagan societies couldn't reach.
The Christian motto: "Those who can, teach."

The Latin alphabet was introduced,
Still in use today. So, don't be seduced
Into thinking these times pre-historic:
The growth of learning was meteoric.

From time to time there were setbacks, of course,
But the Church was a unifying force
In matters legal and political.
In these early years it was critical
For Kings to be well-advised, the law clear.
Although it would still be many a year
Before England was governed by one King,
This was brought closer, to my reckoning,
By great structural changes. To combine
Church and State was the trick. In 669   **669**
Archbishop Theodore of Canterbury
Built a new episcopal hierarchy.
Theo (from Tarsus), enterprising fella,
Brought the English Church under one umbrella.

He created new bishoprics, each see
With its own specific territory,
Yet answerable still to Canterbury.
Our old friend the roving missionary

11

Didn't die out – far from it. Theodore
Established monasteries by the score,
Like the new foundation at Jarrow (Bede's) –
Great temples of learning, serving the needs
Of layman and scholar. Last, but not least,
The parish, with its church and parish priest,
Sprang up from the seeds, few would disagree,
Of this new Theodoran ministry.

Kings needed the Church, of that there's no doubt;
Learning and law they couldn't do without.
Christianity and literacy
Underpinned a King's legitimacy.

This gives a false impression, however.
History's never that simple, never.
Mention of a King's 'legitimacy',
Applied to the late seventh century,
Would have made the venerable Bede laugh.
A better and more fitting epitaph
(Repetition, sorry – no other way)
Is Gildas again: "Wicked tyrants held sway."

Now, back to the plot. Kingdoms, large and small,
Jostled for prominence. One King might fall,
Like Edwin of Northumbria, cut down
By pagan Penda his neighbour, the crown
Swiftly restored to Oswald, who, we've seen,
Was slain in turn by Penda's war machine.
Oswy slew Penda, then, within the year,
Was overthrown by Penda's son, Wulfhere –
Whose successor, near the Trent, in 679, **679**
Won a victory that sealed Northumbria's decline.

'Bretwalda' is a term of Bede's choosing,
To mean an Anglo-Saxon 'over-king'.
Edwin and Oswald (his heroes) qualify,
With Oswy, for the title. I wonder why

Not Penda? Bede was doubtless biased. Still,
Though there was no one English King until
Many moons later, it does indicate
Strong contenders were emerging. The fate
Of the English, by Bede's own reckoning,
Would lie in due course with a single King.

Kings rose and fell according to their wealth,
Their power, prestige and general health –
Hardly, I'd say, the ideal recipe
For constitutional stability.
Moreover, a son didn't inherit
His father's crown by right. No. Strength, merit,
Ambition and brute force, so it appears,
Were used to win the backing of one's peers.

Mercian supremacy grew apace.
The other significant power-base
Was Wessex. King Caedwalla annexed Kent
And Sussex (*circa* 686) and sent   **686**
The Mercians packing. Wessex power
Proved crucial during England's darkest hour,
The Danish invasions, when King Alfred...
But stop. Forgive me. I'm running ahead.

In the eighth century King Ethelbald
Of Mercia, who one old Charter called
"King over all the Southern English", ruled
For forty-one years. Sturdy and well-schooled
In warfare (the Bretwalda of his day),
Ethelbald and his under-kings held sway
Over all England south of the Humber,
Save Wessex; while, in the north, Northumbria
(Bede doggedly finishing his *History*)   **731**
Remained independent. How? A mystery.

Offa was next in the Mercian line.
Charlemagne addressed him as "brother mine",

13

Or "*cher frère*", which he loved (just a tad vain).
Offa was "King of the English". It's plain,
However, this title was self-conferred.
Nice try, Offa, but frankly absurd.

It's clear he liked to demonstrate his strength
By keeping under-kings less at arm's length
Than Ethelbald preferred. Once, with an axe,
He struck off (in a dispute about tax)
King Ethelbert of East Anglia's head!
Wilful or what? The Welsh, too, lived in dread
Of raids from Offa's neighbouring forces,
Some on foot, some storming through on horses.
When the wretched Welsh retaliated,
He went and built this dyke, which they hated.
His 'legacy' in mind (they're all alike),
He named his new creation "Offa's Dyke".

Ethelbald and Offa (no one in between)
Ruled for eighty years, from 716
To 796. That's quite some record.   **796**
Despite the fact they governed by the sword,
As Christians they sought their just reward
In Heaven. What can't be wholly ignored
Is the social progress during their reigns.
Both Kings, to be fair, took the greatest pains
To foster learning and encourage trade.
Fortresses were built, and much progress made
In domestic commerce. Offa's own face
Appeared on the coinage, hardly a disgrace.

After Offa, Mercia's power waned.
His successor, Cenwulf, briefly maintained
Its influence. But Egbert of Wessex,
In 825, subjugated Essex,   **825**
Sussex and Kent. Four years on, Mercia fell,
Followed, we're told, by Northumbria as well.

THE VIKINGS

Too busy keeping one another's thrones warm,
These Kings failed to notice the gathering storm.
The *Anglo-Saxon Chronicle* contains an entry,
Somewhere towards the tail-end of the eighth century,
Where mention is made of "Northmen from Horthaland",
Who arrived in three ships. No one could understand
Their business, but, when challenged (can you believe?),
They responded by butchering the royal reeve.
The *Chronicle* then most helpfully explains
That "these were the first ever ships of the Danes
"To seek out England." Whoever could have foretold
That these attacks would soon increase one thousandfold?

The next raids were isolated affairs,
But caught the English sadly unawares.

Marauding gangs of Vikings came to sack,
Pillage and burn, and seemed to have the knack
Of sniffing out treasure. Lindisfarne, alack,
Was plundered – exposed and open to attack.

Rhyming History

Many a monastery on the east coast
Was vandalised. The poor monks suffered the most –
Some tortured by the wild, rapacious horde;
Some massacred, or sold as slaves abroad.

To the Danes and Norwegians, sea-faring folk,
The Angle (or 'Brit') was a bit of a joke:
Insular, ill-prepared – no mistaking
That rich pickings were there for the taking.
Not just gold and treasure, you understand:
No, the lush fertility of the land
Caught their eye. Being fur-dealers, whalers
And sea-fishermen by trade, these sailors
Were farmers, not after gifts for the wife,
But opportunities for a better life.

The Norwegians (bloody and resolute)
Targeted the north and west, their chosen route
Around Scotland, then down along the coast,
The Scots, Welsh and Irish suffering the most.
The dastardly Danes, on the other hand –
An equally brutal (and brutish) band –
Headed directly for the east, and Kent.
At first, as I've hinted, they too were bent
On death and destruction. But, after years
(Decades) of rape and pillage, it appears
They planned a more organised invasion.
The year 865 marks the occasion.   **865**

Halfdan and his army of 'water-thieves'
Conquered Northumbria. No one believes
It was plain-sailing. He only took York
After fierce resistance. There was talk
Of attacking Mercia. That plan failed.
But one strategy that wasn't derailed
Was the invasion and subjugation
Of East Anglia. Eradication

(Permanent) of two kingdoms in three years
Must have set warning bells a-ringing. Tears,
Meanwhile, were shed for East Anglia's King –
Edmund, earnest, devout, but no weakling,
Cruelly murdered by Halfdan ('the Tartar'),
Ever revered as St. Edmund ('the Martyr').

Next on the list was Wessex. However,
The West Saxons started boxing clever.
Shunning the Anglo-Saxon tradition
Of family feuds, King Egbert's mission
(Remember him? No? Then keep up) was this:
To avoid dynastic 'unpleasantness'
In matters of the royal succession.
So, on Egbert's death, there was no question
But that his son Ethelwulf (with four sons)
Should succeed. When he died, to everyone's
Delight and surprise, the sons remained friends.
The eldest succeeded. No one pretends
That all was exactly sweetness and light,
But these four boys managed, without a fight,
To pass the crown from one to another –
When one died, to the next eldest brother.

By 870, two of them were dead,   **870**
Leaving Alfred (the youngest) and Ethelred
(Now King) to face the Danish force alone.
The precise details may never be known,
But whether or not the Danes were lazy,
Or simply outclassed (reports are hazy),
The West Saxons, at Berkshire Down, put to flight
Halfdan's great army. The undisguised delight
Of every Anglo-Saxon in the land
Was, however, short-lived. Halfdan soon planned
A renewed onslaught and, near Basingstoke,
Routed the West Saxons, whose fate (no joke)
Hung by a single thread. Then Ethelred,
As if this wasn't enough, dropped down dead –

Just like that! Terrible tragedy, true,
But (at the tender age of twenty-two)
Alfred succeeded (unexpectedly)
And, as they say, the rest is history.

ALFRED THE GREAT (871 – 899)

Yet the famous reign of Alfred 'the Great'   **871**
Got off to a shaky start. The first spate
Of light skirmishes with the Danes he lost.
Then, for years, he was obliged (at great cost)
To bribe the heathen hordes to stay away.
Somehow he staggered on from day to day,
Until finally, in 878,   **878**
It appeared that his (and Wessex's) fate
Was sealed. The Danish army had been split:
Half went to Northumbria (Halfdan's bit);
The other (Guthrum's) mounted a huge attack
On Wessex. Alfred's meagre band was forced back,
In disarray, to its most western point yet:
Athelney, in the far reaches of Somerset.

Alfred took stock. Wessex stood alone.
Head on the block, he was now on his own.

Yet the folk of Somerset, one and all,
Rose up, to a man. They answered his call,
Flocking to their King, and serving him well.
Victory beckoned, I'm happy to tell,
For, at Ethendune, the terrible might
Of the enemy force was put to flight:
A miracle, truly, that's what I say,
Given the huge odds. Be that as it may,
The men of Wessex did wonders that day.

Guthrum was immediately baptized.
I suppose it can only be surmised

That he was so overcome (and surprised)
By his defeat (which couldn't be disguised),
That he must have discerned in it, somewhere,
The hand of God. Thereafter, he took care
Not to mess with Alfred. Guthrum agreed,
Rather politely, that there was no need
To interfere with Wessex any more.
Land north-east of a certain line (Danelaw)
Stayed Danish, to which Alfred assented.
The Treaty of Wedmore represented
A blueprint for peace and security,
As Alfred's reign grew to maturity.
Of course, he didn't rest on his laurels.
A wise leader, he knew there'd be quarrels
With neighbours to the west, and with Danelaw.
But this noble King preferred peace to war.

I say 'King'. Though not King of 'England' yet,
I should be quite prepared to lay a bet
That all Saxons, in Danelaw and without,
Saw Alfred as their King, I have no doubt.

19

From now, until his death in 899,   **899**
Alfred's influence was wholly benign.
He translated Bede's massive *History*
Into Anglo-Saxon, a mystery
How he found the time. Apart from its length,
He had to learn Latin, from scratch. His strength,
As a scholar, was his dedication
To literature and education.
He himself wrote books on theology,
On history, warfare and geography.
The *Anglo-Saxon Chronicle* was his
(At least, he commissioned it) and it's this
That marks him out. He exhorted others –
A lesson learnt from his elder brothers –
To harness their energies, pull their weight,
And use their talents to make Wessex great.

Nor were Saxon defences neglected.
Men this side of Danelaw were expected
To help construct forts. A navy was built,
And London garrisoned up to the hilt.

All down to Alfred. Aged fifty, he died.
What of his character? The man 'inside'?
We'll never know, but I'd hazard a guess:
Great in a crisis, good under stress,
Led from the front, but nevertheless
Sensitive, modest and shy of success.

Alfred's successors

Edward the Elder, Alfred's eldest son,
Succeeded, when his father's day was done,
And 'succeed' he did. Not one to panic,
Calm and (like Alfred) strong and dynamic,
He teamed up with his sister, Ethelfled,
To liberate Danelaw. Noble, well-bred,

And honest heirs to their *pater*'s bravery,
They dealt a death-blow to Danish knavery.
In the north-west, formidable and stout,
The 'Lady of Mercia' set about
Engaging the Danes in local campaigns,
While brother Edward mopped up the remains
Of Danish resistance in the south-east.
Their strategy was, at the very least,
To take East Anglia, which they did (with ease),
And press on to the Humber, which (if you please)
They also achieved. It must be admitted
That the Danes by this time were less committed
To fighting than their grandfathers had been.
They'd settled down, and frankly weren't that keen
On risking everything in battle,
Preferring a quiet life, with their cattle.

By the twentieth year of Edward's reign,
Much of the country was 'English' again.
Further north, the Norwegians had a go
At displacing the Danes (919 or so):   **919**
Between these two nations there was little love lost,
As the ill-fated Danes discovered to their cost.

These Norwegians hailed from Ireland. Ragnald –
The old Norse *cliché*: tall (six-foot), blond and bold –
Invaded Northumbria and seized York
With hardly a fight (the Danes were all talk).
Edward acknowledged Ragnald's 'right' (wise man),
But his able successor, Athelstan,
Marched north, recaptured York in 926   **926**
And, as if to prove this was no quick fix,
Eleven years later routed a huge force   **937**
Comprising wild hordes of Welshmen, Scots and Norse.

At this high point in his power, Athelstan
Was King of the English and the Danes. One man,

For the first time, could be called 'overlord'.
But careful, we shouldn't go overboard:
Two years later, Edmund (Alfred's grandson)   **939**
Lost part of what 'King' Athelstan had won.
Olaf Guthfrithson (as his name implies,
Another Norse) captures (surprise, surprise)
York. 'King' Edmund is forced to recognise
'King' Olaf. What happens next? Olaf dies.   **941**

EDGAR (959 – 975)

So, it's 'King' Edmund again. But strong gains
By four successive Kings, over long reigns,
Left their mark. When King Edgar succeeded,
In 959, what England most needed   **959**
Was a breathing space, some stability.
Edgar, a man of grace, ability
And, as luck would have it, sobriety,
Good judgement (I'm a fan) and piety,
Supplied it. A better system of law
Began to emerge as never before.
The Crown reserved (please note: violent times)
The right to try the most serious crimes.
A basic system of criminal law
Thus began to take hold. And there was more:
Edgar's reign witnessed the development
Of more efficient local government.
England, split up into shires (pronounced 'sheers') –
A unit which lasted one thousand years –
Though still one country under a single Crown,
Could be more simply managed from the top down.

Edgar's greatest achievement was the revival
Of the monastic tradition, whose survival,
Most men believed, had been fatally compromised
By the Age of the Deadly Dane. Few were surprised
By gentle Edgar's wise, far-sighted decision
To reform the Church, which he did with great vision.

Edmund, fair to say, started the process
In the early '40s. Nevertheless,
Edgar exhibited particular flair
By building monasteries everywhere.
Based on the order of St. Benedict,
The monks' daily routine was pretty strict –
And a good job, too. Monasteries, one hears,
Had been going steadily downhill for years.

King Edgar's long-postponed coronation   **973**
Resembled more a priest's ordination.
Succeeding at sixteen, Edgar maintained
That thirty (when a priest could be ordained)
Was a fitting age for the anointing
Of a crowned King. He thought of everything.

Who was fit to follow this *Wunderkind,*
A man who seldom strayed and never sinned?
Someone had to, for sadly he was dead
At thirty-two. Edward or Ethelred?
Some choice! Edgar's sons: one feeble, one weak –
Hardly chips off the old block, so to speak.

EDWARD THE MARTYR (975 – 979)

Between the two (scarcely a preference),   **975**
Edward was chosen, out of deference
To age. Ethelred (the little rascal)
Had his brother murdered (at Corfe Castle),
Just four years into his pathetic reign –   **979**
No records, of course; no proof. Then again,
He's hardly likely to advertise, is he?
So began thirty-seven years of misery.

ETHELRED THE UNREADY (979 – 1016)

'Ethelraed Unraed': kindly note the pun.
Dubbed 'the Unready' by everyone

Rhyming History

In succeeding generations, 'Unraed'
In fact means 'the Ill-advised'. So, instead
Of 'the Unready', I put it to you,
It simply means that he hadn't a clue.
Please be aware, then, of at least one thing:
'Ethelraed Unraed' was a dreadful King.

Early on, he managed to muddle through.
Well, if you're a weak King you do, don't you?
But, within a few years, the deadly Dane
Had raised his ugly, hairy head again.
Denmark had a new King, the young 'Forkbeard' Sweyn –
A thorn in Ethelred's side throughout his reign.

First forays occurred once in a blue moon.
But Forkbeard, sensing England's weakness, soon
Ordered regular and repeated raids
On the east coast. Ethelred and his aides,
Cowards to a thegn, offered the Danes money
(This would be sad if it wasn't so funny),
Saying, "Now, chaps, please don't come back again!"
A healthy sense of humour had the Dane.
He merrily launched more widespread attacks,
Accepting 'Danegeld' as a kind of tax.

The inhabitants of the old Danelaw,
Unhappy under Ethelred, now saw
Occasion to side with the invaders,
Seeing them less as marauding raiders
Than long-lost second cousins. Ethelred,
In a state of panic, took to his bed
For seven days, without food or water.
When he got up, he ordered the slaughter
(Imagine) of every single Dane
In the land, then went back to bed again.
Mad, quite mad. Though accounts are distorted,
Mass killings of Danes *were* reported –

At Oxford, for example. Forkbeard Sweyn,
A formidable military brain,
Landed in person, hell-bent on revenge,
Making raids inland as far as Stonehenge.

Ethelred was finished. In 1013   **1013**
He took refuge in Normandy (his Queen
Was Norman). Sweyn, now King in all but name,
Was welcomed in his stead to great acclaim.

The next three years are action-packed. Here goes:
Sweyn died in 1014. The English chose   **1014**
Canute, his younger son, as their new King.
But Ethelred returned and, in the spring,
Drove out Canute (a little ill-prepared),
Who withdrew to Denmark. Not that he cared.
He'd be back. Meanwhile, Edmund Ironside
(Ethelred's rebel son – keep up) defied
His feeble father, invading Danelaw.
The stage was set for all-out civil war,
When Ethelred died (suspicious or what?).
Edmund, who sounds a thoroughly bad lot,
Was declared King. Next, young Canute returned.
Within the year, this noble Dane, who spurned
Peace terms, scored a spectacular success
At Ashington (Essex). This, more or less,   **1016**
Sealed Edmund's fate. As a sop to his pride,
Canute let him keep Wessex. Ironside
Limped off to lick his wounds, and to decide
His next move. Then, luckily, he too died.

CANUTE (1016 – 1035)

Canute ruled for nineteen years, and ruled well.
At times he could be ruthless, truth to tell –
In the early years, at least. First, he wed
Ethelred's widow (smart move). Ethelred
Left three sons. The eldest was soon found dead:

Draw your own conclusions. But a new King
Has to show his subjects he's no weakling –
A murder here and there: par for the course.
Canute, remember, was thoroughbred Norse –
Moreover, an astute politician.
To help consolidate his position,
He surrounded himself with loyal Danes,
But (a clever ploy this) he took great pains
To include in his administration
Senior Anglo-Saxons. The nation
Was divided into Earldoms, not all
Headed by Danes. Now, his choice to install
Godwin in Wessex ('Earl' Godwin to you),
A true-bred Anglo-Saxon through and through,
Raised some eye-brows. But it proved a success –
In the short term, at least. "Never oppress"
Was Canute's *mantra,* and he did his best
To govern by consent, not by conquest.

"Reconciliation" was this King's watchword.
Given his sticky start, you'll think it absurd
When I tell you that one important factor
In his success was as a benefactor
To abbeys and churches. Pagan at first,
Canute converted and showed a real thirst
For all things Christian and religious.
His acts of charity were prodigious.

When, in 1035, King Canute died,   **1035**
It fell upon the Witan to decide
On a successor. Kings were 'made' not 'born',
And the Wise Men of the Witan were torn
Between five choices: Edward and Alfred
(Both in Normandy), sons of Ethelred;
Ironside's infant son, Edward 'Atheling',
(Also in exile); and sons of the late King,
Harold and Harthacanute. A close call.
Edward 'Atheling' wouldn't do at all:

A minor, too risky. The four others
(Through their mother, two brace of half-brothers)
Ranked as possibles. Edward and Alfred
Were thought rather too 'French', too 'Norman-bred',
So the wise Witan chose Harold instead.   **1037**
"You can't go far wrong with a Dane," they said.

Error Number One. Just three years later,   **1040**
Poor Harold was called to meet his Maker.
Harthacanute tried on his brother's shoes:
The Witan offered – he couldn't refuse.
Error Number Two. By 1042,   **1042**
He too was dead. What could the Witan do?
Their old standby – "There's nothing like a Dane" –
Began to sound like a hollow refrain.

Meanwhile, Godwin had been up to no good.
Far from acting as a worthy Earl should,
It's alleged (how often are these things known?)
That, in his efforts to secure the throne
For Harold, he'd had Alfred 'taken out'.
As Ethelred's elder son, there's no doubt
Alfred's claim was strong. But the deed was done,
Leaving Edward as sole surviving son.
Alfred was horribly tortured, his eyes
Gouged out – a gory murder. No surprise
That Edward, therefore, a mild-mannered man,
Was never Earl Godwin's Number One Fan.

EDWARD THE CONFESSOR (1042 – 1066)

So, Edward 'the Confessor' succeeded.
Just at the juncture when England needed
Strong government, political vision
And purpose, they chose him! The decision
Of the Witan wasn't exactly bad:
Edward was the only choice to be had.

Rhyming History

Sadly, though, there was more of the French monk
About him than an English King. He'd funk
Affairs of state, preferring, if you please,
To spend his waking hours upon his knees,
In prayer. Yet, despite his sobriety,
His saintliness and his air of piety,
Our Edward wasn't just a pretty face.
His twenty-four-year reign was no disgrace:
No foreign wars, no Danish invasions,
Little hint, as on former occasions,
Of internal dissent. Earl Godwin, true,
Did flex his muscles. What did Edward do?
He brought in chums from Normandy, wholesale,
While grumpy Godwin groused and prayed they'd fail.
But Edward knew these Normans from his youth:
Churchmen, merchants, soldiers. To tell the truth,
They underpinned King Edward's power-base,
And helped keep surly Godwin in his place.

English craftsmen, too, cried "foul" and "shabby",
When Edward chose, for Westminster Abbey,
Norman architects. This was his pet scheme,
Still, centuries later, dubbed "Edward's Dream".

An enigma, but Edward kept his head
And contrived, at least, to die in his bed.   **1066**
After he'd left for Heaven, however,
All hell let loose. He'd been less than clever
In the matter of his succession. No,
To be fair, the poor chap did have a go
At siring an heir. But his chastity
Could well be the reason (it has to be)
For his lack of success, despite the fact
That he did marry (and here I'll show tact)
Earl Godwin's fair daughter. No great beauty
(Ugly as a frog), she 'did her duty',
Lay there and thought of Wessex, while he prayed:
Not the way that little princes are made.

Edward 'Atheling', son of Ironside
(Remember him?), had regrettably died:
Not exactly a plethora of heirs!
The Norse still viewed the English throne as theirs.
Young Harald Hardrada, hardy, astute,
And direct descendant of King Canute,
Coveted the crown, but bided his time:
Contender the First. Though well past his prime,
Earl Godwin, too, had his eye on the prize,
But he predeceased Edward. No surprise
That his son (Harold with an 'o') reckoned
He could make it: Contender the Second.

There's some evidence that Edward preferred
The English Harold. Contender the Third,
However, was lurking in Normandy:
William, the bastard Duke, and it's he
Who posed the main threat. Ruthless, ambitious,
He waited. The Witan, wise, judicious

And fair, elected Harold. His title
Was tenuous. Their backing was vital.

HAROLD (1066)

Harold, brave and bold, might have borne the brunt
Of one invading army, on one front;
But Harald Hardrada attacked the north,
Just as William was poised to set forth
From Normandy. He was delayed by rain,
Wind and foul weather, and had to refrain
From sailing. This gave King Harold's forces
The chance to march north (they had few horses):
Exhausting or what? Harald and Tostig
(King Harold's traitor-brother, and a pig)
Were met at Stamford Bridge and defeated,
The battle a rout, bloody and heated.

Harald and Tostig both were slain. Good show.
One invading army down, one to go.
Three days later (the end of September –
This is now 1066, remember),
Harold received the news he'd been dreading:
William had landed, last seen heading
Up the beach at Pevensey. He'd arrived.
Harold's soldiers (the ones who'd survived)
Finished their sandwiches, took a deep breath,
Then headed south to keep their date with Death.

The Battle of Hastings

William's forces were well-drilled and fit.
They say he burnt his boats, so couldn't quit.
Moreover (and this was quite inventive),
He offered his men no mean incentive:
After the Conquest, his barons and knights
Were set to share in estate-holding rights,

Each taking a stake in the Duke's success.
They were fighting for land – no more, no less.
Modest in number, disciplined and lean,
William's men, in short, were very keen.

Young Harold, still on something of a high,
Faced the crisis of his life: triumph or die.
King for under a year, and King by right,
His courage was up. He spoiled for a fight.
William, having had weeks to prepare,
Was expecting Harold, but 'when' and 'where'
Were good questions. He could only sit tight
(Spending night, they say, after sleepless night)
And wait. King Harold chose an imposing spot:
Top of a hill (near Hastings). Like it or not,
The Duke (the aggressor) was forced to attack.
Uphill. Against a shield-wall. And on horseback.
Harold's military tactics were very clever.
William couldn't turn back. It was now or never.

From dawn to dusk, a bloody battle raged –
Norman and Saxon, bitterly engaged;
Sword against hatchet, battle-axe on shield.
William attacked. Harold didn't yield.
Anglo-Saxon, heroic to the end,
He had, he knew, his birthright to defend.

So when he fell, an arrow to the eye,
All England mourned, and I shall tell you why.
They loved and feared their King, though few yet understood
Their Anglo-Saxon world had disappeared – for good.

WILLIAM THE CONQUEROR (1066 – 1087)

William had to act fast. Though agile
And astute, his position was fragile.
He accepted Winchester's surrender
With alacrity. Next on his agenda
Was London, England's main strategic city.
Londoners resisted, so, without pity,
William sacked, plundered, pillaged and laid waste
All surrounding villages and towns. With haste,
London surrendered, its civic pride replaced
By abject submission, and a nasty taste
Of what might lie in store for England later.

The Conqueror (or 'Anglo-Saxon hater')
Chose Christmas Day for his coronation.
This event, which should inspire a nation,
Descended into chaos. Shouts and cheers
Inside the hallowed Abbey triggered fears
Outside, among the guards, of high treason;
Whereupon they, without rhyme or reason,
Torched all the houses, causing those inside
To run without. The new King was terrified,
Shaking and trembling, but clung onto his pride:
As coronations go, somewhat undignified.

Domesday Book

A French farce, though hardly hilarious.
The King's hold on power, precarious
From the outset, was maintained by brute force.
Revolt was met, as a matter of course,
With ruthless vengeance. Morcar and Edwin,
Two angry Earls of northern origin,
Tried their hands at rebellion. They failed.
Not only were their private plans derailed,
But every living creature, man and beast,
Between York and Durham in the north-east –
Women, children, cattle, the parish priest –
Were put to the sword, towns razed to the ground.
In *Domesday Book* no record can be found
Of human habitation, just scorched ground –
And that's seventeen years later. *Domesday*
(1086) was the King's special way   **1086**
Of recording land tenure: a survey
Of every hide of land. That is to say
That William, of whom all land was held
(As feudal lord), could collect his Danegeld
(Or tax) according to the land's value.
It also meant, at a glance, that he knew
Which knight or baron owned what realty
(Or estate) – so, who owed him fealty.

An *excursus*. Who today is aware
That freehold land in England, anywhere,
Is still held of the Crown? 'Free' simply means
There's no charge – but the land remains the Queen's.
Nobody 'owns' freehold land. I don't jest.
And that's been the case ever since Conquest.

Back to the plot. *Domesday* proves, beyond doubt,
That Normans were 'in' and Saxons were 'out'.
Thousands of thegns lost their lands. A mere two
English lords feature in *Domesday Book* – true.

William's barons were well rewarded.
Just over two hundred are recorded
In the Book, a true Norman take-over.
Moreover, the Norman-French make-over
Extended to more than matters of land.
French (which few Englishmen could understand)
Became 'the' language. Educated men
Spoke it all the time, only now and then
Switching to Latin as the need arose.
The King spoke it and, as everyone knows,
What the King says, goes. Churchmen from abroad
Replaced the English clergy, their reward
For loyalty and learning. Church music,
And architecture (the English were so sick),
Came under French influence. One major reform
I should emphasise in particular: the norm,
Pre-Conquest, was for legal actions to be brought –
Secular and religious – in the Shire Court.
William had these jurisdictions divided:
Civil cases should be settled, he decided,
In the lay courts, whereas matters spiritual –
Like heresy, marriage and Church ritual –
Were left to the bishops. A basic system of law,
Free from the Church, could prosper now as never before.
William was certainly a bully and a brute,
But his influence on English Law was absolute.

Normandy by right; England by Conquest.
William, I'm sure, did his level best
To juggle both roles, and met with some success.
His family, though, was in a dreadful mess.
Elder son Robert led him a merry dance,
Plotting, openly, with King Philip of France
Against his own father; while the second son,
William 'Rufus', was just out to have fun.
Family squabbles, border disputes, civil war:
Normandy occupied William more and more.

In 1087 he was wounded, badly,   **1087**
Sacking (in a fit of pique) some French town. Sadly,
Neither son was at his side. Robert was away,
Sucking up to the French King, though I have to say
Rufus did turn up (just in time) at the deathbed:
A smart move and politic, it has to be said.

I'd like to draw a line, say "that was that",
But there's a footnote. William was fat
(Obese, let's be honest) towards the end:
Too big for his coffin. They had to send
For six heavy men to sit on the lid.
Another French farce. You know what they did?
They squashed him down, King William the First,
So hard, that his big balloon-belly burst.
I do apologise if I'm giving offence,
But the stench from the explosion was quite intense.

WILLIAM RUFUS (1087 – 1100)

Robert was ready, but England preferred
Rufus. The Church did, anyway. They'd heard
Ugly reports of Robert's treachery,
Rumours of licence, lust and lechery.
Finding William much more to their liking,
They simply invited him to be their King.

So England and Normandy came to be split,
Which the barons didn't like one little bit.
Most found they owed fealty to two masters –
Tricky, to say the least. All the disasters
Suffered by Rufus early in his reign –
Uprisings, revolts, the common refrain –
Stemmed from this uneasy state of affairs:
One inheritance, split between two heirs.

Brother Robert, had he played his cards right,
Might have won the crown with hardly a fight.
But he hadn't the will, just didn't care –
Well, either that or he simply lacked flair.
He missed his moment, and left Rufus alone.
The surly barons could do little but moan.

William the Second didn't turn out
Quite as the clergy had hoped. There's no doubt
He had energy, charisma and charm –
Characteristics that did him no harm.
But he was extravagant, a spendthrift,
Fond of the ladies (if you catch my drift),
Reckless and gay (not in the modern sense),
And ruled, increasingly, at the expense
Of the Church. I should explain what I mean.
The Church had great wealth and, as we have seen,
Church and State were interdependent. The King
Appointed the clergy, and here's the sting:

When an abbot, say, or a bishop died,
The income from his land, from every hide,
Passed, till a successor was named, to the Crown.
This was never actually written down –
It's just what happened, the custom of long use.
It was, however, wide open to abuse.
William milked it for all it was worth.
His hedonistic lifestyle cost the earth.
The longer he delayed a new appointment,
The more he had to spend. The disappointment
(Nay, anger) of the clergy was extreme.
To Rufus, it was just a clever scheme.

How he lasted so long is a mystery.
But stranger things have happened: that's history.

Archbishop Lanfranc of Canterbury
Was the Conqueror's right-hand man. His see
(i.e. Lanfranc's) stood vacant for five years,
While Rufus got through the profits. Then fears
Overcame him, intimations of death.
He resolved, before he drew his last breath,
To repent. Anselm of Bec, though unwilling,
Accepted (to coin a phrase) the 'King's shilling',
Taking on Canterbury. Anselm never
Expected him to live. Rufus, however,
Made (forgive me, this is now 1093)   **1093**
A sudden, unheralded recovery.

For the next four years of William's reign,
He and Anselm were at odds. To explain
The ins and outs were tedious – in brief,
The age-old power-struggle. Anselm's beef
Was royal patronage; the King's complaint,
Episcopal power. Gripping, it ain't!
Finally, Anselm could bear it no longer.
Forced to acknowledge that Rufus was stronger,

By 1097 he had had enough.
He threw in the towel and left in a huff.

In Normandy, brother Robert was bored –
And broke. He was itching to go abroad.
So he pawned (yes, believe that if you will)
His dukedom to Rufus, to hold until
He returned from a trip to the Holy Land.
Even Rufus couldn't wholly understand
His brother's motives: some sort of Crusade
Against Muslims; to call a spade a spade,
What some might call a terrorist attack.
Still, William agreed, till he came back,
To hold the fort. In fact, he enjoyed it –
Managing to recapture, bit by bit,
Land his brother had lost. He loved a scrap.

He also loved hunting. A strange mishap
Occurred in the New Forest one fine day.
Rufus was killed. An accident, some say.
1100, August the second.   **1100**
As I've said, it's generally reckoned
To have been an accident. Oh, by the way,
Brother Henry was in the Forest that day.
I thought I'd mention that. Henry the First,
Who succeeded him. Also at Lyndhurst.
In the Forest. But on another track.
When Rufus got an arrow in his back.

Fratricide? Don't be so absurd.
Assassination? Mum's the word.

HENRY BEAUCLERC (1100 – 1135)

Like his father and grandfather before,
Henry acted with speed. He knew the score.
A man of talent and intelligence,
I'm sure that none of you will take offence

When I suggest that arrow was no bad thing:
For Henry the First was an outstanding King.
Nicknamed 'Beauclerc' (or 'Clever Scholar'), he knew
Exactly what a wise monarch had to do.
A mere three days later, his coronation
Took place at Westminster. Years of stagnation
Under Rufus were swept away. Anselm
Was recalled. With two strong men at the helm
Of Church and State, the barons were satisfied
Of the prospects for peace. They were pacified
By a new Charter of Liberties. This King,
It has to be said, thought of everything.

This kept the barons sweet when Robert, the swine
(Devious as ever, corrupt and malign),
Now back from murdering Muslims, decided
To stake his stale claim. The barons divided
Fifty-fifty (give or take). Though he hated
Rotten Robert, Henry negotiated.
When the Duke landed (1101),   **1101**
It came as no surprise to anyone
That the coward had no stomach for a fight.
He pleaded exhaustion; and money was tight.
The devil demanded; the bargain was made:
Two thousand pounds *per annum*. This Henry paid.
Two grand a year! For England! A mere pittance.
Robert slunk back to Normandy. Good riddance.

This tribute was paid for only five years.
The two split states gave rise to renewed fears,
Among the barons, of instability.
Henry showed political agility:
He made a challenge to Robert at Tinchebray,
In 1106. I do have to say,   **1106**
This was a bold move. It was make or break.
Nobly, he risked his life for England's sake.
Robert resisted, but to no avail:
He languished the next thirty years in gaol.

Henry Beauclerc had never been stronger,
And ruled a full twenty-nine years longer.
In view of recent events, his main obsession
Was to seek to secure the royal succession.
He married Matilda, a Scottish princess.
This grand union was a stonking success.
Anglo-Scottish relations (never much fun)
Blossomed. Queen Matilda bore Henry a son,
Little Prince William, a most welcome heir,
And elder brother to Matilda 'the Fair'.
But Henry's pride and joy was shipwrecked at sea,
In 1120. No male progeny   **1120**
(Legitimate, at least) survived. Poor Henry,
Distraught, never recovered from the tragedy.

Now he concentrated on his daughter.
Keeping the lass well away from water,
He schooled Matilda in affairs of state,
And married her (1128)   **1128**
To Geoffrey Plantagenet, aged 14 –
Geoffrey, that is. Matilda wasn't keen.
Geoffrey was son to the Duke of Anjou.
Lately, there'd been a great deal of to-do
Between Anjou and Normandy. In fact,
If it hadn't been for this marriage-pact,
Normandy might have been ripe for invasion –
Though, fortunately, not on this occasion.

Church matters. Relations with Anselm were frosty:
The Norman campaigns were exceedingly costly.
Church revenues yet again seemed to fit the bill,
As they had in Rufus's time – a bitter pill
For the clerics to swallow. Quarrels by the score
Raged between Church and State. Enough. I'll say no more.

Sadly, Henry rowed with his son-in-law.
It wasn't exactly a state of war,

They just didn't get on. Matilda, too,
Seemed to wind him up. And these were the two
He'd groomed to succeed him. When Henry died,   **1135**
He left a fine old mess. Poor fellow, he'd tried
To secure a smooth succession. But, frankly,
All he managed was family anarchy –
A doleful legacy for a skilful King.
It just goes to show: you can't plan anything.

STEPHEN (1135 – 1154)

Geoffrey and Matilda may well have been
Henry's nominal heirs, but, as we've seen,
These things depended on personality
(And chance), rather than on strict legality.
Stephen was Henry's nephew. When he heard
His uncle was at death's door, he conferred
With chums, who told him the barons preferred
Him to Matilda. Stephen seized his chance.
Geoffrey and Matilda were stuck in France.
He hopped over the Channel (no time to waste)
And headed for London with indecent haste,
Where, with some dodgy promises, he won
The hearts and minds of its people. That done,
He proceeded to the capital city,
Winchester, where his brother (more's the pity)
Was Bishop. So that, too, was a walk-over.
He then took advice, and went to talk over
Affairs of state with the late King's Chief of Staff,
Robert of Salisbury, who could only laugh
At the prospect of Matilda on the throne.
A woman? Pah! (Sexism is how it's known).
So, Robert gave Stephen his full support:
The Crown this thief had so fervently sought
Was his. Poor, bleeding England paid the price:
Stephen was, as they say, not at all nice.

Amazingly enough, the King's first few years
Were peaceful. It was sure, though, to end in tears.
Poor Stephen proved to have an uncanny knack
Of giving offence. Salisbury got the sack,
And brother Henry flew into a rare old tizz
When passed over (he'd assumed it was his)
As the new Archbishop of Canterbury:
Foolish and wilful decisions – very.

It took four years for Matilda to arrive.
It beats me how ditherers like this survive.
Four years! Leaving Geoffrey in Anjou (fine),
She landed, in 1139,   **1139**
To claim her inheritance. 'The Empress'
(As she liked to be called) failed to impress.
Feeble Stephen, almost immediately,
Was handed a golden opportunity
To have her imprisoned. Misplaced chivalry
Inspired the fool to let her go. French, you see,
An odd lot, they *will* do things differently.
I'd have locked the baggage up, had it been me.

She repaid Stephen's 'generosity'
By having *him* arrested (treachery)
At the battle of Lincoln, in '41.   **1141**
Stephen, if you please, given the chance to run,
Offered himself up. It defies belief.
Matilda, fortunately, came to grief:
Wilful and vain, she contrived to upset
All of London. How stupid can you get?
She could have been crowned Queen, simply no doubt,
Instead of which the people threw her out.

Stephen was released (a hostage exchange).
For seven dreadful, long years little changed.
They slugged it out, Stephen and the Empress,
While England suffered. A terrible mess.

Some barons exploited the civil war
To rob the wealthy and abuse the poor.
Private armies, torture and starvation –
Poverty, cruelty, deprivation.

In 1148, thank the Lord,   **1148**
Matilda threw in the sponge. She was bored.
In Normandy the Angevin faction,
Led by Geoffrey, had won power. Action
By Stephen was quite out of the question.
Matilda retired (Geoffrey's suggestion)
To Normandy, a far more restful life,
To fight like any normal man and wife…

…Until, that is, 1151.   **1151**
Geoffrey of Anjou died; his day was done.
He left an heir, another Henry, his son
With Matilda. Popular with everyone –
Clever, strong, approachable, never vain –
Henry wed Eleanor of Aquitaine,
By which union, you should understand,
He annexed a vast acreage of land
(Comprising central and south-western France)
To Normandy. You could say, at a glance,
That Henry owned the best land on the map.
Being an enterprising sort of chap,
He thought he'd like a shot at England too,
And so (surprise, surprise) what did he do?

He summoned up his army, sailed over,
And challenged Stephen, who just keeled over –
Metaphorically, at least. Stephen's heir,
Eustace, had died. The King was in despair.
The barons, too, were almost at their wits' end:
They found it harder and harder to defend
Their miserable monarch. To save face,
They allowed him to reign, without disgrace,

For life, adopting Henry as his heir.
Both signed on the dotted line, then and there:
The Treaty of Westminster, the greatest thing
Stephen had done since the day he was crowned King.
The date: 1153. He was tired.   **1153**
Drained. Exhausted. In '54 he expired.   **1154**

A competent soldier, no politician,
The central irony of his position
Was the succession. After years of bloodshed and strife,
This was secured. His uncle would have given his life
For such an outcome. Henry died bruised and battered.
To him, the succession had been all that mattered,
Whereas when Stephen died, who couldn't have cared less,
A successor was ready to clear up the mess.

HENRY THE SECOND (1154 – 1189)

Henry the Second quickly set about
A programme of radical reform. Out
Went a baron's right to wage private war. Out
Went his right to build unlicensed castles. Out
Went his right to bear arms against the King.
Beckett, a name *not* to the barons' liking,
Was Henry's right-hand man in this campaign,
Ruthless and efficient: no pain, no gain.

Henry's chief domestic pre-occupation
Was root-and-branch law reform. His creation
Of a system of King's Courts throughout the land
Led to uniformity, on the one hand,
In jurisprudential administration –
One standard, for the first time, for one nation –
And, on the other, a new sense of fairness:
A 'Common Law', coupled with an awareness
Of the King's personal responsibility
For the promulgation of justice. It was he,

The Romans to the Wars of the Roses

Henry himself, out of his private Treasury,
Who financed prisons and courts, and the salary
Of each of the King's Justices. The expense,
Given the scale of these reforms, was immense.

Henry developed (this was still quite new)
The jury system: 'twelve good men and true',
Fledgling and rudimentary but, hey,
Rome, remember, wasn't built in a day.
Replacing the dreaded Trial by Ordeal,
Juries enjoyed huge popular appeal.

Legal reform had a direct effect
On religious affairs, as you'd expect.
The clergy, whatever their crimes, were tried
In the Church Courts. Now, few people denied
This was somewhat unjust – priests judging their peers.
It was just something that had gone on for years,
But not, for Henry, a good enough excuse.
Determined, as ever, to stamp out abuse,
He prepared the ground by appointing his friend,
Beckett, to Canterbury – and to this end:
The new Archbishop, his place-man, would now vote
With Henry on every issue of note,
Including the 'crimes-of-the-clergy' question.
Thomas à Beckett balked at this suggestion –

Rhyming History

But not until after his appointment
Was ratified. The King's disappointment
(Call it fury) knew no bounds. Livid, irate,
He declared all Beckett's estates confiscate.
Thomas fled the country, some say in tears,
And stayed in exile for the next five years.
Henry himself was made of sterner stuff:
He'd done his best, but enough was enough.

Other matters craved the King's attention –
Abroad, for example. I should mention
That out of his thirty-four-year-long reign
He spent just a third in England. The strain
Of holding all his widespread realm together
Never troubled him, whatever the weather.

But his four sons were a pain in the arse
(Pardon my language) – another French farce.
The eldest, Henry, he groomed to succeed
As next King of England, but felt no need
To give him a proper job. An error.
The second, Richard, was a right terror.
Despite Henry's promise of Aquitaine,
He spat in his father's face. Then again,
He'd been left in limbo, without a job,
Just like his brother. Geoffrey was a slob
(The third son). Brittany, in the north-west,
Was his promise. But, when put to the test,
This too proved to be a bit of a con,
With no power attached. Youngest son, John,
Was Henry's little pet, though strangely, as such,
Only got Ireland, which irked him very much.
Four ambitious boys, all angry and idle,
Drove their poor father almost suicidal.

The murder of Thomas à Beckett

To add to his troubles, Beckett came back:
Henry soon found himself upon the rack.
To the unalloyed joy of the whole nation,
The King had organised the coronation
Of his eldest son (and heir) as co-regent.
Sowing doubt and discord (such was his intent),
Thomas roundly denounced this new 'arrangement',
Setting the final seal on the estrangement
Between Henry and his former best friend.
Where, the people wondered, would it all end?

"Will no one rid me of this turbulent priest?"
Cried the King. Those were his very words, at least
So we are led to believe. Four foolhardy knights
Took it upon themselves to set the world to rights.

In 1170, the 29th of December,   **1170**
A date the whole of Christendom will ever remember,
Thomas à Beckett, in his own Cathedral, was struck down,
A victim of the bizarre conflict between Church and Crown.
Thomas à Beckett. 'Saint' Thomas. Thomas 'the Martyr'.
His murder was a public relations disaster.
Poor Henry. Though his throne was never in doubt,
He performed public penance, ever devout.

The King ruled for another nineteen years.
In truth, he'd shed mainly crocodile tears
Over Thomas's untimely demise.
Henry himself, to general surprise,
Suffered few ill consequences. He reigned
With wisdom and justice. All England gained
From his continuing reforms: in law,
Finance and government. Even the poor
Enjoyed a respite, albeit quite brief,
From baronial tyranny. Light relief
In this oasis of peace came from France:
French songs (or *chansons*), poetry and dance.
The 'new-age' baron, freed from feudal strife,
Enjoyed more leisure to spend with the wife.
Castles gave way to manor houses. Knights
Took up fox-hunting and other delights,
Such as jousting and politics (art, even),
Pastimes undreamt of in the time of Stephen –
Quite a turnabout, I'm sure you'll agree.

Henry had his fair share of tragedy.
His son and heir expired in '83,   **1183**
Followed three years later by young Geoffrey.   **1186**
Richard and John led him a merry dance,
Plotting and bickering. Philip of France
Got his claws into Richard (not as strong
As cracked up to be), stringing him along
Into an alliance against his father.
This worked the old King up into such a lather

That he died in '89, a sad and broken man,   **1189**
Still popular with his people (but then, I'm a fan).

RICHARD COEUR DE LION (1189 – 1199)

The next decade saw Richard comfortably in charge,
Though more often than not he was absent, at large
On the Continent, or away on Crusade.
In those days, that's how reputations were made –
As knight-errant, adventurer, romantic.
Now call me old-fashioned (or worse, pedantic),
But the King became an absentee-landlord,
Never happier than when wielding his sword
In the Holy Land. One year into his reign,   **1190**
He left for Jerusalem, on which campaign
He was joined by Philip of France, his old chum;
Leopold of Austria, who'd only come
To stir up trouble; knights and barons galore;
And ardent Christian zealots by the score.

It does strike me as singularly odd
That crusaders *will* invoke their own God
As the one and only. Be that as it may,
Richard '*Coeur de Lion*' set sail. On his way,
He acquired a wife, a lovely princess
Named Berengaria. Nevertheless,
She bore him no issue. Lionheart wasn't keen
On the opposite sex (if you know what I mean).

Richard and his boys (read nothing into that)
Sought to liberate, from Saladin's *diktat*,
The old City of Jerusalem. They failed.
Despite this ignoble fact, Richard was hailed
As a hero. He won some skirmishes, true,
But was obliged, in 1192,   **1192**
To conclude with Saladin a temporary truce.
All that bloodshed for nothing. I ask you, what's the use?

49

Rhyming History

Meanwhile, Richard had quarrelled with Leopold –
Insulted his banner or something, we're told.
So, travelling home, later the same year,
He was forced to disguise himself, for fear
Of arrest. He dyed his beard burnt sienna
And shaved his head. But, passing through Vienna,
He was spotted by spies and apprehended –
Not quite what the brave Lionheart intended.
He languished the next fifteen months in prison,
Till the English made the painful decision
To ransom their King for a vast sum – in cash:
One hundred and fifty thousand marks! Most rash.
Only two-thirds of this was paid. Nevertheless,
It did seem a lot to ease a vain King's distress.

On his return, in 1194,   **1194**
He had himself crowned again, just to 'make sure'.
He feared his position had been compromised
By his wilful neglect, and I'm not surprised.

Was he grateful? You've got to be joking.
You'll find this, I'm sure, just as provoking
As I do. He left England for ever!
He knew, at best, he'd been less than clever.
In his long absence he'd lost land to France.
He reckoned that he stood an honest chance
Of salvaging his battered reputation,
By striving, with savage determination,
To recover his lost terrain. Five years
It took him – but it still ended in tears.
Fighting Philip of France, now his sworn foe,
He suffered a mortal wound. Death was slow.

Richard *Coeur de Lion*, forty-two, expired
In 1199. Loved and admired   **1199**
By his loyal subjects, a Christian hero –
Popularity: ten; accomplishments: zero.

Ten long years. So, who kept Richard's throne warm?
Luckily, his father's thirst for reform
Was kept alive by one man, Hubert Walter,
England's Chief Officer, who didn't falter
In his firm resolution to keep the King's peace.
His strong stewardship saw the common wealth increase.
He sustained King Henry's tradition of just laws.
There was also a welcome and popular pause
In the ongoing struggle between Church and State,
For Walter was Archbishop too. He threw his weight
Behind local government reform. He believed
In elected officials. Mayors were conceived,
And aldermen – new posts, still with us to this day.
He granted Charters to towns. Such was Hubert's way.

JOHN (1199 – 1216)

John had been his father's favourite son.
'Lackland', as he was known to everyone,
Was the nickname Henry had given him.
Two-faced, incompetent and rather dim,
'Lacklustre' might be a fitter epithet –
For John was, frankly, our most dismal King yet.
Succeeding the Lionheart in '99,
He turned his back on England (not a good sign)
For the first five years, seeking to enforce
His Angevin dynastic rights. Of course,
He failed. Normandy, Anjou, Maine: all were lost,
As the hapless John discovered, to his cost,
That (a) keeping your land is far from easy,
And (b) crossing the Channel makes you queasy.

By 1204, he'd done all he could to earn   **1204**
His nickname. His sole option was to return
To England. Hubert Walter, still going strong,
Was holding the fort. Hubert could do no wrong
In my book. But in 1205 he died.   **1205**
This set the country on a downward slide.

John began his sorry domestic reign
By inflicting maximum fiscal pain
On his subjects, rich and poor. Clerical and lay,
Barons and burghers, all classes were made to pay.
The barons, in particular, took great offence
At this blow to their pride. Their anger was intense.
They, in turn, passed this new burden of taxation
Down to their own feudal tenants. The vexation
This engendered at all levels was obvious,
Though John appeared to be blithely oblivious.
Or was he? Draining the barons of their wealth,
He contrived to invest in the Crown, by stealth,
Greater autocratic authority. This scheme
Was one of which other tyrants could only dream.

I'm exaggerating. Johnny needed the cash,
Simple as that – not so much devious, as rash.
His foreign wars had bled the coffers dry.
He needed funds from somewhere, which was why
He raised the rates. He raised some hackles, too,
And later got his come-uppance – sad, but true.
Part of the barons' undoubted ill-humour
Stemmed from an unproven (though likely) rumour
That John had played a most unsavoury part
In the murder of Prince Arthur. 'Little Art',
As he was fondly known, was Geoffrey's son
(John's elder brother), loved by everyone –
Barely a child, but John's nephew, therefore
A rival for the throne. Need I say more?

John picked a quarrel with the Pope, whom he hated.
Innocent the Third, a complex man, berated
The King over some episcopal appointment.
John, unable to contain his 'disappointment',
Let rip, and was forthwith excommunicated. **1209**
John was highly chuffed, for this *impasse* created
A vacuum in Church business. Very good news!
Services were suspended, and all revenues

He nicked for the Crown. The stalemate rumbled on
For five fruitful years: game, set and match to John.
By 1214, this wastrel King had itchy feet.   **1214**
He wanted his French lands back, but suffered defeat
At the Battle of Bouvines. The cost of this war
(Huge) meant John had fewer funds than ever before.

Magna Carta

The barons were revolting (John's joke, not mine),
And in 1215 forced the poor King to sign   **1215**
Magna Carta, by the Thames, at Runnymede.
This great Charter, it's fair to say, sowed the seed
Of Civil Liberties in Britain to this day.

"No freeman shall be imprisoned, taken away,
"Exiled, or otherwise destroyed in any way
"Except by the lawful judgement of his peers
"Or the law of the land." For eight hundred years

Rhyming History

Magna Carta has stood the stern test of time –
A solid constitutional paradigm
In rocky reigns, like that of Charles the First,
When royal tyranny was at its worst.

The Charter prevented John raising feudal dues
Beyond what law and custom permitted. Good news
For the taxpayer. John, renowned for his short fuse,
Could huff and puff all he liked, but couldn't refuse.
"No taxation without representation,"
A cry that's gone up from the British nation
Over the years, isn't out of the Charter –
But the contract John signed was a good starter.

The King no longer stood above the law –
That's it in a nutshell. Never before
Had limits on his power been spelt out
Quite so explicitly – without a doubt,
A major landmark. The country as a whole
Supported the barons' efforts to control
The Crown. Stephen Langton, Archbishop of Canterbury,
Offered his backing. Freemen. Londoners. Everybody.

Innocent the Third (I told you he was odd),
In his own name (and, I suppose, that of God),
Suddenly became chummy with Johnny again,
And encouraged the idiot King to refrain
From implementing the Charter. So, John swore
At the barons and carried on as before.
This, you can well imagine, was the last straw.
Determined finally to show John the door,
The barons resigned themselves to civil war.
They offered the crown to Louis of France (Philip's son),
When suddenly, to the relief of everyone,
John collapsed and died in October the same year.
Sad to say, no Englishman shed a single tear.

HENRY THE THIRD (1216 – 1272)

He left a mess. Henry, his eldest son,   **1216**
Was just nine. The country was overrun
(Some parts, at least) with marauding French troops.
England had to jump through several hoops
Before peace was restored. Civil unrest
Was averted. Good men (the very best)
Formed a Minority Council: Pembroke,
Langton, de Burgh, together brought to book
Many a rebellious baron. Even France
Became a lesser priority, with no chance
Of (or inclination for) winning back lost land.
Their sober caution is easy to understand.

They drove out Louis, the French interloper.
Henry, however, was a born no-hoper.
A pleasant enough chap, with a charming wife,
He seemed to have a knack of stirring up strife.
At twenty-five, he himself assumed the reins   **1232**
Of government and sacked de Burgh. All the gains
Achieved during the Regency (not without pain)
Were wilfully cast aside and flushed down the drain.

His wife's family (French) he quickly promoted.
This caused resentment among those he demoted.
For the next twenty-six years he just muddled through,
But it was, I'm afraid, a case of *déjà vu* –
The barons *versus* King John, an action replay.
Ignoring the Charter, he went badly astray
In one particular agreement with the Pope.
Without consultation, Henry (the utter dope)
Offered to buy Sicily for his second son –
From the Pope! To the surprise of everyone
(Quite apart from the price, which was huge), he agreed
To pay off all Innocent's debts. He felt no need
To check how much His Holiness owed. I forgot,
Sicily had to be conquered first. Not a lot,

You'll agree, to be said in favour of this pact.
Simon de Montfort, a baron of no great tact,
But blessed with the talents and skills that Henry lacked,
Cut up quite rough about all this, and that's a fact.

Simon de Montfort

A relative of the King's (on his wife's side),
De Montfort was a man of passion and pride.
In former days Henry's special favourite,
Simon had come to observe how, bit by bit,
The King was growing too powerful again.
"Attend to your subjects!" (that constant refrain)
Was reaching fever-pitch by 1258.   **1258**
Simon and the barons, ever more irate,
Forced a showdown. Henry the Third was constrained
To acknowledge everything England had gained
By *Magna Carta* – indeed, rather a lot more.
The King, facing the real threat of civil war,
Was obliged to sign the Provisions of Oxford,
Under which he and the barons, with one accord,
Agreed to regular meetings of 'Parlement' –
Quite revolutionary, as far as it went.
Though light years from the body we know today
As our Parliament, it still went some way
Towards a basic accountability.

De Montfort displayed a rare facility
In the dark arts of the political game.
His Privy Council governed in all but name.
Henry remained nominally in control,
But de Montfort's Parlement assumed the role
Of the monarchy. In effect disenfranchised,
Poor Henry was a broken man, demoralised,
Angry and sad. But de Montfort soon realised
These were unchartered waters, and wasn't surprised
When the royal party began to fight back.
Within a few years, he was under attack

From the King's son, Edward. Longshanks, they called him.
Tall and lanky, folk had dismissed him as dim
In his early youth. Just shows how wrong you can be,
For at Lewes, in 1264, it was he   **1264**
Who challenged de Montfort on the battlefield.
Wounded and weary, Edward refused to yield.
He branded de Montfort the foulest traitor,
Resented the wrongs done to his dear *pater*,
And resolved to fight to his very last breath.
Fortunately for England, he escaped death
And was taken prisoner with the old King,
Who'd turned up too, in armour and everything.

De Montfort was destined for a sticky end.
Young Edward was sprung from prison (by a friend)
And fought Simon at Evesham in 1265.   **1265**
This time he resolved not to be taken alive.
A fight to the death! De Montfort's best remembered
For his Parlement. But Simon was dismembered
After his Evesham defeat, which just goes to show
That decency still had a long way to go.

Henry the Third suffered sorely from the strains
Of office. After Evesham, he passed the reins
To Edward. Increasingly senile and weak,
The old man half-abdicated, so to speak.
In 1270 Edward rather put paid   **1270**
To Henry's hopes by setting off on Crusade.
The fragile King somehow managed to muddle through
Till his death, not before time, in '72.   **1272**

EDWARD LONGSHANKS (1272 – 1307)

Edward was proclaimed King in his absence:
The obvious choice, it made perfect sense.
In his latter youth wilful and headstrong,
Arrogant and vain, he could do no wrong

After Evesham – courageous and loyal,
Fearless and gallant, the perfect royal.
Handsome, to boot, with loads of sex appeal,
He wooed, and won, Eleanor of Castile –
A woman of good sense and sound judgement,
Who inspired respect wherever she went.

Returning at his leisure in '74,   **1274**
Edward harboured a healthy respect for the law.
The King recognised the value of 'Parlement',
And decided to consult (well, to some extent).
Simon de Montfort, his adversary and foe,
Had, for all of his shortcomings, his head screwed on, so
Edward encouraged constitutional debate.
He understood the risks of leaving it too late
To settle grievances. A talking shop (no more),
'Parleying' was preferable to civil war.

There was just one Assembly in those early days,
Not unlike the modern House of Lords, in some ways.
Enthroned in full pomp and splendour, the King presided
Over barons and clergy. He alone decided
Policy, legislation and judicial redress.
His authority was absolute. Nevertheless,
He recognised the value of consultation.
A very early form of representation
Was also introduced. Knights from the shires,
Burghers from the larger towns, even squires,
Were summoned to attend – the eyes and ears
Of the English nation. Over long years,
They became the Commons, with their own Speaker,
Growing in strength as Lords and Crown got weaker.

Edward was a prolific legislator.
The laws he passed are a true indicator
Of his thirst for reform. In 1285   **1285**
(The Statute of Winchester) he began a drive

The Romans to the Wars of the Roses

To build and nurture, through new legislation,
A system of law enforcement for the nation.
In the same year an impressive Act was passed
(The Statute of Merchants), which addressed, at long last,
The concerns of commercial traders. Their trust,
Edward came to appreciate, was a must.
He wooed the middle classes with great success,
By reforming, root and branch, the whole process
Of debt collection. It's anybody's guess
Exactly how much misery and distress
Were suffered in debtors' prisons in future years,
But they were widely welcomed, or so it appears.

Though on the home front Edward scores loads of points,
In foreign affairs his record disappoints.
True, he conquered Wales (if you call that a good thing).
For eight years he dedicated everything
To his Welsh campaigns – money, energy, manpower.
The political atmosphere, of course, turned sour
When he had to raise taxes to finance it all –
But the merchant classes adored him, so played ball.

The job was well done. The Welsh were first defeated
In '77, and the task completed,
After the odd rebellion, in '83.
Llewelyn ap Gruffydd fell in battle. It was he
Who caused our Edward most grief. He had a brother, see,
Called Dafydd, who fought to the last, valiantlee.
Poor Dafydd was captured, put on trial, and later
Tortured and executed, a most foul traitor.

Edward excelled himself on the battlefield.
He was even known to fight without a shield.
"The best lance in the world", a plucky fighter,
He never got wounded, the lucky blighter.

But the King's hot-headedness led him astray,
With dismal consequences felt to this day.
In 1290 Queen Eleanor passed away.   **1290**
She was much lamented, which isn't to say
That Edward wouldn't have behaved the same way
Had his Queen outlived him. Be that as it may,
Edward the First launched his first Scottish campaign.
God alone knows what the madcap hoped to gain
By this crazy scheme, beside personal glory,
But it was badly botched, and the outcome gory.

The Hammer of the Scots

Anglo-Scottish relations had been pretty fair
Till Scotland was suddenly left with no male heir.
In 1286 Alexander the Third died.
Well, it was worse than that. He went out for a ride:
Foul weather; thick fog; zero visibility.
He rode his steed straight off a cliff and into the sea.

His wee granddaughter, Margaret, was his sole heir –
The so-called 'Maid of Norway', with lovely fair hair,
Blue eyes, a gorgeous smile, but only four years old.
Her succession was guaranteed, or so we're told,
But when, in 1290, little Maggie died,
The Scots called upon our Edward to decide
The succession. John de Balliol he chose,
A broadly popular choice. There soon arose
Disputes, however. Crowned in 1292,   **1292**
John paid homage to Edward (the latter's due),
But Edward, bully that he was, insisted
On overall control. When John resisted,
Backed by his Scottish lairds, on full independence,
The 'Hammer of the Scots' invaded. John's defence
Of his kingdom was courageous and resolute,
But sadly in vain. Warfare was Edward's strong suit,
And by 1296 conquest was absolute.   **1296**
This bloody campaign (a charge that few would refute)
Led to long centuries of bitterness and war
Between two peoples who, just a few years before,
Co-existed in harmony under the law.
Edward the First has a great deal to answer for.

Adding insult to Scotland's dire misfortune,
Edward had the Coronation Stone at Scone
Removed to Westminster, and was proclaimed King.
That was that, he thought. He'd done everything
To secure his position. But at Stirling,
The following year, a Scottish uprising,
Headed by William Wallace, put to flight
The English. A man of terrifying might,
Ferocious courage and rare tactical skill,
Wallace cut swathes through the enemy, until
No man was left alive. In 1298   **1298**
Edward staged a comeback, and could celebrate
Victory at Falkirk. Life wasn't easy,
However, and not until 1303,   **1303**

Rhyming History

After six awful years of bloodshed and pain,
Could Edward boast that Scotland was his again.
Stirling was recaptured in 1304,   **1304**
But (and you may well ask) what was it all for?

Wallace was executed (call him a traitor)
In 1305, but, barely one year later,   **1305**
Robert the Bruce emerged as Scotland's new hero,
Reducing Edward's 'accomplishments' to zero.
In 1306 Bruce was crowned King – hurrah!   **1306**
Poor Edward, former legislator and star,
Buffed up his armour and sallied forth again
For Scotland, his reputation down the drain.
He died in 1307, near Carlisle,   **1307**
Unwilling, perhaps, to go that extra mile.

A sad waste. Focused, talented and strong,
In his heyday Edward could do no wrong.
The 'English Justinian' he was called,
Lawmaker *extraordinaire* – but he stalled.

Every political career, they say,
Ends in failure. Well, be that as it may,
Even the tame barons turned against him.
Plans to defend Gascony, on a whim,
Were vetoed. Edward was left high and dry.
They refused their support. Do you know why?
Taxation. Financing the Scottish wars
Had proved ruinous, costing tens (no, scores)
Of thousands of pounds. Relations, too, were strained
With the clergy and merchant class. All he'd gained
In his youth, in his dotage he cast aside.
When, aged sixty-eight, still fighting, Edward died,
He bequeathed a respect for the Rule of Law.
But the stage was set for years and years of war.

EDWARD THE SECOND (1307 – 1327)

Those who tired of Longshanks certainly never reckoned
On that miserable, wilful wimp, Edward the Second.

A child psychologist would have a field day.
Weak son of a strong father, possibly gay,
Wanting his share of parental affection,
It's hardly surprising, upon reflection,
That Edward should seek solace in close friends (male) –
Conduct, in that macho age, beyond the pale.

One Piers Gaveston soon caught the King's eye.
Edward was captivated, and here's why.

Piers was tall and slim, with dark chestnut hair,
Of graceful gait, charming and debonair.

His well-fashioned hose was in perfect taste,
Showing to fine effect his slender waist.
You get the picture. Gaveston was smart,
And flattered his way straight to Edward's heart.

The barons resented the King's *amour*,
But Piers was pushing at an open door.
Edward was entranced, in truth he was lost.
He worshipped Gaveston, but at what cost.
In 1311 the barons met,   **1311**
Demanded the exile of the King's 'pet',
And sought in future to restrict his right
To promote his darlings. Without a fight,
Edward succumbed. Gaveston was banished.
Overnight, it seemed, the problem vanished.

But Edward's agreement hadn't been real:
He'd had his fingers crossed, the imbecile.
So, Piers returned. The barons cut up rough.
They'd been thwarted. When the going got tough,
They could be ruthless, and they'd had enough.
Dispensing with justice (just legal stuff),
They contrived Gaveston's execution –   **1312**
The only step, short of revolution,
They could take to curb the wilful King's powers.
Edward, when he heard the news, howled for hours.
Frenzied, distracted, they feared for his life.
They sent for Queen Isabella, his wife –
He was married, didn't I say? She tried
To comfort her husband, but he just cried,
Sobbed his little heart out: "Piers! Oh, my Piers!"
Months later, he was still in floods of tears.

England's weakness was, of course, Scotland's strength.
Bruce was prepared to go to any length
To cast off the much-despised English yoke.
Edward led his army (this is no joke),

In 1314, up to Bannockburn,   **1314**
And there events took a terrible turn.
Bruce and his sidekick, Douglas, a crack team,
Drove the English into the 'burn' (or stream).
Pursued at spear-point into the water,
Edward's forces suffered wholesale slaughter.
Of archers and cavalry, that fateful day,
Fewer than one man in eight escaped the fray.

Scottish independence was won at a price.
I won't bang on about it, let this suffice:
For the next two hundred and fifty years,
Give or take, Scotland (or so it appears)
Was wracked with blood-feuds, assassination
And feudal anarchy – a sad nation,
Divided and ill-used. National pride
Was purchased at a high price: suicide.
This is a controversial point of view,
Of that I'm aware. Without more ado,
Therefore, I shall return to my main theme:
King Edward, and his lack of self-esteem.

As you'd expect, Eddie's reputation
Stood at an all-time low. The whole nation
Held its breath. The King was at the mercy
Of the barons, who courted controversy
By openly jockeying for position.
His cousin Thomas sought his deposition,
Though he, in his turn, faced stiff opposition
From moderates. A long war of attrition
Was fuelled by Edward, who'd unwisely begun
A fresh liaison. Hugh Despenser (and his son)
Were the new favourites. In 1322   **1322**
Lancaster (Thomas) staged a military *coup.*
He failed. Proud and brutal, a villain through and through,
He proved himself unpopular, and stupid too.
If he'd played his cards right... Well, that's speculation.
His execution gave rise to jubilation.

Rhyming History

Though Lancaster had given cause to curse,
The Despenser *régime* was far, far worse.
They exploited the King, body and soul,
Abused his trust and were out of control.
The Queen, in particular, resented
The two new interlopers. "Contented"
You couldn't call Isabella. "Stoic"
Would be more appropriate. "Heroic,"
Better still. But this was the final straw:
Marital peccadilloes, civil war –
All rather more than she had bargained for
When she became Longshanks' daughter-in-law.

And then Mortimer gave her the glad eye –
Roger Mortimer, exile, alleged spy,
Recalcitrant baron and Edward's foe.
Isabella's knees turned to jelly, so:
When Edward, in '25, was away –   **1325**
Some French diplomatic mission, they say –
Isabella became Mortimer's mistress.
She didn't deliberately cause distress
To Edward. She couldn't help herself, see.
She'd had a hard time. Between you and me,
He must have seen it coming. Anyway,
The Queen made some excuse, a holiday
Or some such thing, and fled abroad. Invasion
Was planned (another *coup*). On this occasion,
The perpetrators had the full support
Of barons and clergy. People all thought
It was time for a change. Edward's young son
(His namesake), popular with everyone,
Was even said to be in on the act.
A lad of wisdom, discretion and tact,
He kept a low profile. Deposition
Of his own father made his position
A trifle dicey. Not since the Conquest
Had a King been deposed. He did his best

To keep calm. King Edward was overthrown
In autumn 1326. It's known   **1326**
That Edward the Third ascended the throne
In 1327. It's *not* known,   **1327**
Exactly, what became of his poor dad.
There's no doubt his fate, though, was pretty bad.
Bullied, tearful, in a terrible state,
Half-frantic, he was forced to abdicate.

Edward died in prison later the same year –
A nasty, uncomfortable death, I fear.
A red-hot poker came into it, some say…
For more details, see Christopher Marlowe's play.

EDWARD THE THIRD (1327 – 1377)

Young Edward was a mere lad of fifteen
When he ascended the throne. As we've seen,
He kept a cool head. He bided his time.
He turned a blind eye to his mother's crime
(As he saw it) – her long-standing affair
With Mortimer. He exercised some care
To shun any mention of regicide.
Ambitious and able, he took great pride
In his grandfather's memory, old Longshanks.
Edward inherited, for which he gave thanks,
His granddad's political *antennae*, so
He determined that Mortimer had to go.
Not in the least averse to playing dirty,
Edward, at Nottingham, in 1330,   **1330**
Arrested the traitor in the dead of night
And arranged his swift execution. The fright
All but killed Isabella, but, thereafter,
Edward could feel he'd avenged his poor father.
The old Queen's influence waned, and the new King,
At nineteen, felt far less of an underling.

The Hundred Years' War

England soon drifted into war with France.
Drifted! For one hundred years! At a glance,
There were three main causes. Firstly, the French
Were strongly pro-Scottish, which gave offence,
Of course, to the English. Edward was keen
To reconquer Scotland, which, as we've seen,
His father had lost. When Robert Bruce died,
It didn't take Edward long to decide
To seize the initiative. Bruce's heir,
David, was a mere lad, and it was rare,
In those tough times, for a child to succeed.
Edward took his chance and with lightning speed
Drove wee David out, placing on the throne
One Edward Balliol, a complete unknown.
David fled to France (he, too, bided his time),
Whence, some twelve years later, and now in his prime,
He returned home in triumph. Philip, the French King,
Gave his full backing – arms, men, ships, everything.
Edward was livid, the English forced to withdraw:
Reason Number One for the Hundred Years' War.

Reason Number Two: Gascony. This province
(French) had been English ever since, since… well, since
Anyone could remember. Edward the Second,
Even at rock bottom, nevertheless reckoned
On good old Gascony, down in the far south-west,
To yield an income. Its value was manifest:
A wine-growing region of the highest worth,
In an age when decent *vino* cost the earth.

Quite simply, France wanted Gascony back.
King Philip the Sixth developed a knack
Of harrying the English. Philip insisted
On his right to the province. Edward resisted.

Reason Number Three: in 1328
The last Capet King of France died. From that date,
Edward staked a doubtful claim to the French Crown –
Through his mother, Isabella. A showdown
Was inevitable. All-out war began
In 1337, and ran and ran,   **1337**
Like an old French farce, for the next hundred years,
On and off. Hugely popular, it appears,
With the English at home (who hated the French),
There's precious little to be said in defence
Of this crazy conflict. When it finally finished,
English influence, if anything, was diminished.

Edward made a poor start. Attempts at invasion,
In 1339, failed. The first occasion   **1339**
For joy came in 1340, when the French fleet,   **1340**
At Sluys, suffered an inglorious defeat.
But naval victories were of limited use:
England was soon forced to negotiate a truce.

The Black Prince

1346 saw a new phase of the war.   **1346**
With his son the Black Prince at his side (who men swore,
At sixteen, to be "of Chivalry the Flower"),
King Edward celebrated his finest hour.
At Crécy, his army scattered the French forces.
The latter, in heavy armour, and with horses,
Fell before Edward's secret weapon, the long-bow.
The English archer was a formidable foe:
From Crécy, right through to the field of Agincourt,
Years later, it was "Us Archers Wot Won The War!"

A well-directed arrow could pierce plate-mail.
Disciplined, fearless, the English couldn't fail.
They loved warfare. The chronicler Froissart wrote:
The English will honour their King (and I quote),

"Only if he be a lover of arms and war
"Against their neighbours". Edward, like no King before,
Embodied this profile. He loved a fight:
The archetypal, perfect, royal knight.

Edward laid siege to Calais (after Crécy),
A tricky task (and not a little messy).
Twelve months it took for the town to surrender –   **1347**
Our troops were on enemy soil, remember.
Any fool will tell you, when all's said and done,
That being the aggressor isn't much fun.

Calais served as HQ for future campaigns.
Otherwise, there were few significant gains.
Isolated 'victories' in Gascony,
Occasional 'successes' in Brittany,
And that was it. Pathetic. Hardly worth
The effort, I'd say. And it cost the earth.

Lack of funds forced Edward, in September,
To conclude another truce. Remember,
Edward was popular at home, a star.
Yet all he really had was good PR.
So, he could pass off defeat as victory –
That age-old trick, the spinning of history.

The Black Death

The King returned home in triumph, his stock
At an all-time high. However, a shock
Of seismic proportions was set to break –
This time not a political mistake,
But an Act of God. The 'Great Mortality',
So-called, carried off, in its totality,
Over one third of the population.
The Black Death devastated the nation.
Spread in all probability by rats,
Off the ships, it struck down aristocrats

And serfs alike, the poor and the wealthy,
Though (strange to say) the young, fit and healthy
Were the most at risk. The rats carried fleas,
Who hopped off their hosts and spread the disease.

The plague first surfaced in 1348,　　　　　　　**1348**
In Dorset, and spread at an alarming rate
Across the south. The graveyards of Somerset
And Devon were soon full to bursting, and yet
The Death raged on. Fields and open spaces
Were used as makeshift burial places.

In terms of human misery and grief,
The great 'visitation' defied belief.

As London succumbed to the disaster,
The plague swept further north, ever faster.
Some towns and villages were left without
A single living inhabitant, without doubt
A huge, humanitarian catastrophe.

Perceived, however, demographically,
This sudden decline in the population –
The 'slimming down', as it were, of the nation –
Doubled the cost of labour at a stroke.
The peasant, your average working bloke,
Could command higher wages. His rent fell
And, if he played his cards right, he did well.

The surviving landowners, conversely,
Were wrong-footed, and suffered adversely.
The spectre of the deserted village,
With its dearth of labourers, meant tillage
(Or ploughing) of the land came very dear.
Rather than lose more income, year on year,
And suffer nervous stress from loss of sleep,
Landlords changed the user of their land to sheep.

"Every cloud…" as they say. Trade in wool,
For centuries, kept England's coffers full.
The Death, a clear expression of God's wrath,
Simply encouraged men to weave more cloth.

The closing months of 1349   **1349**
Showed mortality rates in sharp decline.
A bitter winter (snow, ice, a big freeze)
Killed off billions of plague-ridden fleas.
Hundreds of thousands of rats simply starved
Or froze to death, their numbers more than halved.
The human survivors drew a deep breath,
Buried their dead, and cocked a snook at Death.

War

Profits from the export of raw wool soared.
Sales to Flanders, the prime market abroad,
Boosted the funds for Edward's new campaign
In France. Oh, yes – the war was on again!

The Romans to the Wars of the Roses

In fact, the horrors of the pestilence
Proved a mere short-lived inconvenience.
Hostilities resumed, though little more,
To be honest, than skirmishes – the war
Gently simmering over a low flame,
Rumbling on, more of a courtly game,
Played out by knights, than serious action.

Hardly surprisingly, the reaction
Of the nobles at home, given the cost,
Was sceptical. The war hadn't been lost,
Exactly, but men began to question
Its objectives. The merest suggestion
Of withdrawal drove Edward to fury.
The King, remember, was judge and jury.
He held absolute sway. But he took the point.
Ever solicitous not to disappoint
An uneasy nation, he raised the stakes.
"Never apologise for your mistakes"
Was Edward's *credo.* So, in '55,   **1355**
His French campaign went into overdrive.

His first forays out of Calais, his base,
Failed miserably. Fearing loss of face,
If not outright military disgrace,
He wisely decided to play his ace.

Edward the Black Prince was now in his prime –
At twenty-five, the hero of his time.
The premier warrior of his day,
The Prince led our army at Poitiers
To perhaps the most famous victory
In English medieval history.
Though some will complain that I exaggerate,
1356 was a seminal date.   **1356**
The French feudal forces were outflanked, their fate
Sealed by our brave bowmen. Edward the Great

(For had not the Prince died prematurely,
He would have been dubbed 'the Great', most surely)
Restored his father's fading reputation,
Winning the plaudits of a grateful nation.

Philip the Sixth's successor, John the Second,
Was captured. But it's generally reckoned
The English made a pig's ear of the treaty.
Punch-drunk on victory, and far too greedy,
They badly overplayed their very strong hand,
By forcing the French to give up so much land
That the people repudiated the peace,
Spat on the truce, and demanded the release
Of their King. Edward, in person, let it be known
That his 'hereditary right' to the French throne
Was above negotiation, and besieged Rheims,
Where he planned his coronation. "In your dreams,"
Was the citizens' response, and no expense
Was spared in their stout and spirited defence
Of that fine, ancient Cathedral City.

Edward, rebuffed, soldiered on (more's the pity)
And marched into Burgundy. There his success
Was hardly more marked. By degrees, the stress
Of these foreign wars was starting to show.
All very fine had he been winning – but no:
As doubts at home were beginning to grow,
Edward, in 1360, sued for peace. So,   **1360**
The Treaty of Calais was ratified.
Both sides, apparently, were satisfied
As follows: Edward renounced (yet again)
The French crown, in return for Aquitaine.
After nearly twenty-five years of war,
One's entitled to ask again, what for?

Edward's decline

Edward's fortunes deteriorated fast.
The Calais treaty wasn't built to last.
Plague broke out afresh. Aquitaine was lost.
Ever more burdensome, the massive cost
Of these idle campaigns weakened the King.
Increased taxation left men wondering
Where it would all end. Even the Black Prince
Was losing his touch. It was ages since
He'd enjoyed a success. Dejected and tired,
This flower of English chivalry retired
From the French wars in 1371.   **1371**
The ill-starred exit of his warrior son
Was a cruel set-back for Edward. His wife,
Moreover, his consort, the light of his life,
His best belovèd Queen Philippa, had died
Just two years earlier. It can't be denied
That he never recovered from this twin blow.
Edward, however, was no quitter, so
In 1372 he set sail,   **1372**
In person, for France – yet to no avail.
Foul weather struck. He never got over.
His fleet was left stranded, stuck in Dover.

Domestic squabbles also plagued the King.
Two of his sons couldn't stop quarrelling –
John of Gaunt and the Black Prince the culprits.
They never saw eye to eye. The deep splits
In Edward's family, one supposes,
Sowed the seeds of the Wars of the Roses.

But I'm in danger of running ahead.
By '76, the Black Prince was dead.   **1376**
Edward, distraught, hung on for one more year.
He clung stubbornly to life, his one fear
That the crown should pass to his little grandson,
Richard, before his majority. No one,

But no one, wanted a Regency again.
Edward the Third, however, struggled in vain.
Within twelve months, the intolerable strain
Had taken its toll, and his majestic reign,
Half a century long, staggered to its end.

I'll make no serious effort to defend
Edward's foreign policy. Yet, on the whole,
He won the respect of his subjects. His role,
His mission, was to lead. The burdens taxation,
In good times and bad, imposed upon the nation
Were shouldered by the people (who despised the French)
With fortitude. Parliament did sometimes blench
From backing their monarch, but he was listening,
They sensed, to their cause. A wise, pragmatic King.

Language, law and culture

A footnote. Ever since the Norman Conquest,
French was deemed the official language. At best,
English (at least among the educated)
Was frowned upon as second-rate and dated.
Spoken, of course, the length and breadth of the land,
Simple English was considered far less grand
Than *la langue française*. The French wars, however,
Meant this snobbery couldn't last for ever.
An Act passed a few years after Poitiers,
Banishing French from the courts, had this to say:
Since the French tongue was "much unknown in this Realm"
And for years past had threatened "to overwhelm"
Our legal system, in future "all pleading
"And judgements spoke by men of law and breeding
"Should be spoke in English – in the mother tongue".
Though a few crusty lawyers stubbornly clung
To legal French, here was a revolution.
Schoolmasters followed suit. The evolution
Of the English language developed apace.
Just as Norman-French (post-Hastings) took the place

Of Anglo-Saxon, so the vernacular
Now replaced French – and truly spectacular
Was the transformation. Within a few years
Came the Chaucers, the Gowers, and the Shakespeares,
Then the Miltons and Marvells (poets by the score),
Their humble beginnings in the Hundred Years' War!

RICHARD THE SECOND (1377 – 1399)

When Richard the Second, son of the Black Prince,
Succeeded his grandfather, it was years since   **1377**
An underage monarch had sat on the throne –
1216, to be precise. It was well known
What a wretched time poor Henry the Third had,
When, aged nine, he succeeded King John, his dad.
Richard, at ten, was barely one year older,
But, as a character, stronger and bolder
Than Henry. This augured well. Nevertheless,
His government depended, for its success,
On his guardians. His uncle, John of Gaunt,
Whose hatred of the Black Prince would come to haunt
England for generations, sat at the head
Of Richard's Minority Council. Instead,
However, of heeding the old King's mistakes
In the failed French campaigns, he too raised the stakes.
Nor were these all that he raised: the final straw
Was a new tax imposed to finance the war,
Levied per head (a 'poll tax') of one shilling.

The Peasants' Revolt

By 1381, few men were willing   **1381**
To pay this 'Evil Subsidy'. An assault
On the Establishment (the Peasants' Revolt),
By a poor and disgruntled population,
Threatened the very fabric of the nation.
The rebels, mainly from Essex and from Kent,
Converged on London, recruiting, as they went,

Bands of discontented followers. They sacked
The houses of the justices; they attacked
And set fire to prisons; they stormed the Tower.
Richard, in what some called his finest hour,
Rode to meet the insurgents. Picture the scene:
The King of England, a mere lad of fourteen,
At Mile End, on horseback, alone, facing down
Thousands of rebels, in defence of his crown.

Unfaltering of voice, he pledged to redress
All proven grievances. He promised access
To his ministers. Pardons were guaranteed,
With fairer taxation according to need.
Promises of feudal emancipation
Were offered to peasants across the nation.
He was cheered to the rooftops! Most noble King!
But Richard's cynicism was sickening.
Not one pledge did he honour. And no prizes
For guessing the outcome of the Assizes.
Rebel agitators were hanged by the score,
The price for stirring up the truculent poor.

Richard's character

King Richard was haughty, stern and capricious –
His subjects, in turn, cautious and suspicious.
Men had to "bend the knee" (by Royal Decree)
In the King's presence, and call him "Majesty".
Richard's adolescent immaturity,
His deep-seated sense of insecurity,
Led to bitter feuds with his uncles. Woodstock
(Edward's youngest son, no chip off the old block)
And his brother, old John of Gaunt, resented
Their nephew's new 'favourites', and lamented
Their own dwindling influence. They reckoned
Their grandfather's spirit (Edward the Second)
Was returning to haunt them. His sorry reign
Looked set to be played out all over again,
Unless they took prompt and radical action.

Chief 'pet' and leader of the King's faction
Was the Earl of Oxford, Robert de Vere.
A snob, whose nickname at Court was "Sir Sneer",
The Earl was not the only acolyte
Who flattered Richard's ego. None too bright,
He nonetheless divined the quickest route
To the King's heart, and others followed suit.

In the mid-eighties matters came to a head,
As discontent with Richard's advisers spread.
The French threatened invasion. England's defence
Required new levels of taxation. Sound sense,
One might have thought, in the face of such a threat.
Edward the Third would have done the same, and yet
Parliament, flexing its muscles, resisted,
Impeached Richard's Chancellor, and insisted
That the King defer to its authority.
Richard, having almost reached majority,
Declared these resolutions treasonable,
Unconstitutional, unreasonable

And void. His opponents retaliated
With ruthless determination. They'd waited
Far, far too long for this opportunity.

Few royal 'friends' escaped with impunity.
Some were exiled, some even executed.
King Richard submitted. He attributed
This treachery to his uncles. He was right.
De Vere of Oxford put up a feeble fight
At Radcot Bridge, but his forces were routed.   **1387**
Gaunt headed the opposition. Few doubted
His ambition, along with that of his heir,
Henry, Earl of Derby, who played his fair share
In testing the King's fragile authority.
But Richard was no fool. His priority
Was to hold fast to his badly battered crown.
Proud to the last, he had the sense to back down.

Over the next two years, with consummate skill,
He rebuilt his damaged power-base until,
In 1389, he reasserted   **1389**
His broken authority. He averted
Further confrontations, and began to reign
With greater force of character. His campaign
In Ireland, the first for some two hundred years,
Was deemed a triumph, while he put paid to fears
Of invasion by wooing, with some success,
Isabella of Valois, a French princess.
There followed a welcome period of peace,
Which survived poor Richard's premature decease.

So, what went wrong? Character will out, they say,
And Richard's petulant nature won the day.
There remained sundry old scores to be settled.
The 'divinely ordained' King was still nettled
By the interference of his elders, so
Uncle Woodstock, he decided, had to go.

Murdered. His own flesh and blood. Into exile
Went other opponents, the highest profile
Of whom was his cousin, Henry Bolingbroke,
Earl of Derby. The Duke of Norfolk (a crook)
Picked a quarrel with Henry. Along the way,
Richard got involved (it's all in Shakespeare's play)
And took advantage of their angry dispute
To banish both parties. Rather less astute   **1398**
Was his foolish decision to confiscate,
When John of Gaunt died, the whole of his estate,
Which, by law, passed to Henry, his son and heir.

Abdication

Richard's moment of madness didn't end there.
Almost immediately, he turned his back
On England, by leading a renewed attack
On Ireland. Henry Bolingbroke seized his chance,   **1399**
Coming home to reclaim his lands. His advance
Was swift and spectacular. Richard returned,
And nonchalantly announced to all concerned
His resignation. His abject surrender
In favour of his cousin, 'the Pretender',
Took even Bolingbroke by complete surprise.
We shall never know, we can only surmise,
But maybe Richard, a born self-publicist –
Psychologists have called him a narcissist –
Knew the game was up. Public abdication,
In a blaze of glory, caused a sensation.
In martyrdom he found his true vocation,
A kind of triumphant humiliation.

Henry Bolingbroke became Henry the Fourth.
Strong support, particularly in the north,
From families like the Percys, guaranteed
That Henry's cause, not Richard's, would succeed.
The King himself (or 'ex-King', I should say)
Was sent to Pontefract without delay.

Rhyming History

A cell in the Castle served as his quarters,
Where he starved to death (on Bolingbroke's orders?).

The worst of endings to a tragic career.
An infant King, crowned in his eleventh year,
Instantly popular, a handsome young chap,
Smart and intelligent, Richard's handicap
Was his Regency Council. Gaunt (mean, jealous,
Unimaginative and over-zealous)
And Woodstock (incompetent, interfering,
Arrogant, treacherous and domineering)
Were a deadly duo. Richard was smothered
And stifled. He never fully recovered.
So, I blame his elders. He hadn't a chance.
Mark, nonetheless, his achievements: peace with France,
Facing down the Peasants' Revolt (at fourteen),
And champion of the arts, by which I mean
Patron of Gower and Chaucer, whose finest verse
Was written during his reign. Things could have been worse.

HENRY THE FOURTH (1399 – 1413)

Henry of Lancaster, he of the Red Rose,
Though strong, was less safe than he liked to suppose.
He enjoyed a doubtful legitimacy
As the new King. Richard left, more's the pity,
No heir. But Henry, as old John of Gaunt's son,
Had as good a case, he claimed, as anyone.
Others disagreed: a seven-year-old boy,
The Earl of March, could, pundits argued, destroy
Henry's right. The little Earl was descended
From Edward the Third's second son, the splendid
Lionel of Antwerp, whereas John of Gaunt
Was only Edward's third son. This came to haunt,
As we shall see, England for generations,
As disputes between these angry relations
Led to the Wars of the Roses. But, for now,
King Henry the Fourth faced the music – and how!

Thirty-three years old, determined and strong,
Henry, in his own eyes, could do no wrong.
Confident, single-minded, the new King
Nonetheless understood that everything
Of which he stood in sole possession
(His kingdom) was a tainted succession.
Where cousin Richard had harboured delusions
Of grandeur, Henry had no such illusions.

Within months, a plot to assassinate   **1400**
The King at Windsor, and to reinstate
His deposed cousin, was foiled. The plotters –
Rutland, Huntingdon and other rotters –
Were engaged (and killed) at Cirencester.
King Richard was still living, remember.
But shortly afterwards, at Pontefract,
He died. I'd be wholly lacking in tact
If I implied the responsibility
Was Henry's – but it's a possibility.

Rhyming History

There followed hard on the heels of this plot
An uprising in Wales. Like it or not,
The Welsh had guts. Their man of the hour,
The charismatic Owen Glendower,
Rallied his fellow countrymen with his dream
Of an independent Wales – a hare-brained scheme
If ever there was one, but bold nonetheless.

Early on, his efforts met with some success.
He joined forces with formidable allies,
Like Edward Mortimer, who (surprise, surprise)
Was uncle to the Earl of March, who, we've seen,
Was next in line to the throne. Owen was keen
(Or so he said) for the young Earl to succeed –
Provided Welsh autonomy was agreed.

The Percys jumped ship around 1403,   **1403**
Joining up with the Welsh. Between you and me,
Lord Henry Percy, Earl of Northumberland,
And his son Hotspur were getting out of hand.
Effective 'Kingmakers' to Henry the Fourth,
They wielded huge influence across the north.
They reckoned their power would prosper and grow,
Following Bolingbroke's *coup d'état,* but no.
Henry refused to defer to any man:
Bad news for the Percys and their master plan.
They threw in their lot with Owen Glendower,
A new alliance of frightening power.
Henry, with his trusty son Hal at his side,
Took this challenge to his kingship in his stride.
He faced the rebels head-on, as was his way,
And his forces, at Shrewsbury, won the day.

The fiery, hot-tempered Harry Hotspur fell,
Mortally wounded. His father (absent) did well
To escape with his life. His blatant treason
Was pardoned by the King, for some strange reason.

Though well-intentioned, Henry quickly regretted
His show of clemency. Aided and abetted
By Scrope, Archbishop of York, the elder Percy
Threw this ill-advised demonstration of mercy
Back in the King's face by rebelling again,
A mere two years later. But this new campaign
Was doomed. In 1405, at Shipton Moor,   **1405**
Henry, in top form, showed the rebels the door.
Scrope was executed as a foul traitor.
Northumberland escaped, but, three years later,
Was hunted down and killed. Owen Glendower
Fled to the hills. His men, now a sad shower,
Struggled on. But Henry had the upper hand,
A force to be reckoned with throughout the land.

During these troubled times the war with France
Flared up yet again. The French took a chance,
Allying themselves with the Welsh. The Scots, too,
Were restless. Scots, French and Welsh: a lethal brew.
Henry picked off his enemies one by one.
The war against the Welsh was as good as won
When their staunch ally, the Scots' King James the First,
Fell into English hands. Well over the worst,
Henry consolidated his position
With an Anglo-French truce. No politician
Worth his salt depends on martial force alone.
After eight years, Henry had secured the throne.
By 1408, he could start to relax.   **1408**
Only one thing kept him awake at night: tax.

But Henry the Fourth, the wisest of Kings,
Knew when to listen to his 'underlings'.
The King could compromise. He kept a cool head.
He waged war on all fronts, but died in his bed…

…Sooner than he expected. 1409   **1409**
Saw the start of Henry's physical decline.

His long, slow illness was a strange mystery:
Syphilis, some whispered, though no history
Could be discerned in the royal family;
Leprosy, some opined. The reality,
I think you'll find, is that at forty-seven   **1413**
Poor Henry was more than ready for Heaven.
His energy sapped by years of civil war,
The old man's time was up, and he knew the score.

His quartet of fine sons wept at his bedside:
Hal, Thomas, Humphrey and John. Thousands outside,
Tens of thousands, mourned the passing of their King.
If Henry was honoured for any one thing,
It was for bringing peace and stability
To a divided kingdom. His legacy
(Prince Hal's inheritance) was patent to see.
In 1413 the stage was finally set
For King Henry the Fifth. You ain't seen nothing yet!

HENRY THE FIFTH (1413 – 1422)

Tales of Hal's wild youth are exaggerated.
Cultured, industrious, well-educated,
He could read (and write) in the vernacular –
In a King, little short of spectacular.
At sixteen, he assumed overall control
Of his father's flagging Welsh campaign, a role
That he discharged with such dynamic and drive
That when he came to succeed, at twenty-five,
He'd already acquired the kind of vision,
And experience, that his new position
Required. Within a year of his accession,   **1414**
A plot which challenged his right of succession,
Fomented by Henry, Lord Scrope of Masham,
Was crushed in typically robust fashion.
Thereafter, the old 'Ricardian' faction
Afforded the King little cause for distraction.

The Romans to the Wars of the Roses

Henry the Fifth's brief reign was dominated
By war with France. Treaties negotiated
By his cousin and, to a lesser extent,
His father were torn up. The King was hell-bent
On conquest. Even the Treaty of Calais,
In which Edward the Third (after a bad day)
Had renounced his long-held claim to the French crown,
In return for Aquitaine, was dusted down
And found wanting. Old Angevin holdings (Maine,
For instance, even Normandy and Touraine),
In addition to our old friend Aquitaine,
Were put on the list, along with other lands
Which had never even been in English hands.

What motivated Henry? Perhaps he'd learnt
From his own father, who'd had his fingers burnt
By squabbles born of internal division.
War-mongering abroad was a decision
More to do with cynicism than morals –
Busying "giddy minds with foreign quarrels,"
As Will Shakespeare, a fellow poet of mine,
Puts it so succinctly in his play. Well, fine,
If you reckon trouble at home's an excuse
For invading a sovereign state. Abuse,
I call it: abuse of position, of trust,
Of due process. This craven cry of "needs must"
Is cowardly and crude, and holds no water –
A pitiful excuse for wholesale slaughter.

Yet Harry's a hero. History says so.
And history never lies, so on we go.

Charles the Sixth of France was past it, half-insane –
A sad figure, quite frankly, and a tad vain.
Not a bad man, he underestimated
The full extent to which the French were hated
By the Brits. Loathed. Despised. By 1415,   **1415**
The whole nation was fired up, hungry and keen

To have a crack at 'the frogs', their age-old foe.
By August, they were bursting to have a go.

With an army of 11,000 men,
Henry invaded Normandy. One in ten
Succumbed to deadly sickness. Decimated,
The army soon rallied, and celebrated
An unexpected victory at Harfleur.
The French, despite this hard blow to their *honneur,*
Reckoned that in human terms the greater cost
Fell on the English, who were thought to have lost
Half their forces in battle, or to disease.
The brave survivors were ready, if you please,
To fight on. Henry preferred a change of tack:
Strategic withdrawal rather than attack.

He marched (via Agincourt) towards Calais,
But encountered a huge force blocking his way:
Over 20,000 French, some mounted knights.
Our lads were outnumbered four to one. By rights,
It should have been a massacre, and it was –
But the other way round! And this all because
The French, on horseback, lacked the mobility
Of our English archers, whose agility
And fleetness of foot gave them the upper hand.

The Battle of Agincourt

The French, advancing through water-logged land,
Quickly got bogged down. Imagine the scene:
Massed ranks of bowmen, agile, fit and lean,
Facing heavily-armoured horsemen stuck,
Up to their fetlocks, in slush, mud and muck.
Sitting targets! As the first French knights fell,
More horses piled in behind them, pell-mell.
Five thousand English archers drew their bows
And the rest, as every schoolboy knows,

The Romans to the Wars of the Roses

Is history. Before the French could draw breath,
Our brave boys waded in and hacked them to death.

Enemy losses defy credibility:
Twelve members of the senior nobility;
Fifteen hundred knights; and, from the more humble ranks,
Nearly five thousand men-at-arms. Henry gave thanks,
Of course, to God. Why the Almighty chose our side
(The underdog, perhaps?), I'll leave you to decide.
But we did enjoy divine support, quite clearly,
For, while the perfidious French suffered dearly,
We lost fewer then five hundred and fifty men.
Thanks, God! It's good to know, every now and then,
That England can count on Your support. Anyway,
On October the 25th (St. Crispin's Day),
The famous English victory at Agincourt
Altered the entire course of the Hundred Years' War.

Thousands of enemy prisoners were taken,
On the King's orders. Unless I'm much mistaken,

God was napping when Henry, whether mad or bored,
Had dozens of these wretched souls put to the sword.
"All's fair in love and war" is a vile expression,
Calculated to plunge me into deep depression.

Henry now had the bit between his teeth.
Spurred on by blind ambition, self-belief
And sheer luck (a deadly combination),
He achieved in time the subjugation
Of Normandy and, by 1419,   **1419**
Had taken Rouen. But his war machine
Was stalling. The fact that it took five years
To get this far gave rise at home to fears
That the whole enterprise would end in tears.
England needn't have worried. It appears
The French had learnt nothing since Poitiers,
And things continued to go Henry's way.

By 1420, the French were forced to concede.   **1420**
In May a peace treaty was finally agreed:
The Treaty of Troyes. King Henry was recognised
As heir to the Valois throne, and few were surprised
When marriage to Catherine, the fair French princess,
Sealed the deal and crowned the triumphant King's success.

The Dauphin, however, the French King's rightful heir,
Kicked up a rare old fuss. He didn't greatly care
Who married his kid sister, but this agreement
Made Henry, during Charles' lifetime, the Prince Regent.
I mean, losing the succession was bad enough,
But this added insult... He flounced off in a huff,
Refusing to recognise the validity
Of the Troyes treaty. Vanity, stupidity,
Call it what you will, but the Dauphin's denial
Put the new Prince Regent, as it were, on trial.
Henry had to fight on. The Dauphin's position
(Like his character) was weak. French opposition

Had, nonetheless, to be met head-on and snuffed out.
By now, however, with no shadow of a doubt,
Henry, in his mid-thirties, was feeling the strain
Of his unrelenting, seven-year-long campaign.

In 1422, at yet another siege,   **1422**
Henry fell victim to dysentery, a disease
That killed him within weeks: a sad and sorry end
To a glittering career. I cannot pretend
To admiration of this war-mongering King,
But his military skills were astonishing.
Dying young at thirty-five, he accomplished more
On the field of battle than any King before.
Spectacular success in France! He won the war!
Sorry to be a killjoy, folks, but again – what for?

HENRY THE SIXTH (1422 – 1461; 1470 – 1471)

As successor to his new two-nation stronghold,
Henry left a baby son barely ten months old:
Henry the Sixth of England and Second of France.
The poor little fellow. He didn't stand a chance.

In the early years of this infant King's reign
His uncle Bedford managed the French campaign,
Scoring at Cravant, in 1423,   **1423**
A long-forgotten but vital victory.

Joan of Arc

Doggedly pushing south to Anjou and Maine,
He was stopped in his tracks by a hurricane:
Joan of Arc. The so-called 'Maid of Orléans',
A simple peasant girl, still in her teens,
She heard voices exhorting, "The French army
Needs you, girl!" Of course, they thought she was barmy –

But she pulled it off. In 1429 **1429**
This divinely-guided visionary called time
On the English. Despite Bedford's resistance,
Joan of Arc, at Orléans, with God's assistance,
Routed our forces. The Almighty changed sides!

The Dauphin was crowned at Rheims (quite a surprise) –
King Charles the Seventh. The French, newly inspired,
Went from strength to strength. And the English were tired.
Confidence at home wavered. Lack of success
In the field led to a certain restlessness
In Parliament, and among our allies.
Even Bedford (no fool) came to realise
The game was up. In 1435 he died, **1435**
Leaving the poor, faint-hearted Henry to decide
On a course of action. A placid, passive man,
He sued for peace. An abortive process began.
Unproductive attempts, over several years,
To reach a compromise always ended in tears.

The Duke of Orléans, a prisoner-of-war,
Taken alive shortly after Agincourt,
Was freed in 1440. The elusive peace   **1440**
Was not secured, however, by the Duke's release.
A fresh attempt to keep diplomacy alive
Was made when the young King, in 1445,   **1445**
Married the French Queen's niece, Margaret of Anjou.
Poor Henry wasn't too keen, but what could he do?
La belle Princesse formidable was quite a catch.
As King, he couldn't very well decline the match.

This 'alliance' proved to be of little use,
Leading (at best) to a temporary truce.
Henry might have preferred to stay single. Instead,
He admitted a termagant into his bed.

The next step in the King's admirable campaign
Was his bold offer of territory in Maine –
No preconditions, and in good faith. I say 'bold'
Because his war-obsessed magnates (both young and old),
Landowners in France, lacked the imagination
To grasp the fact that no reconciliation
With their French neighbours could conceivably take place
Without some loss of occupied terrain – and face.
Henry's peace-bid failed. The French took this as a sign
Of intransigence and, in 1449,   **1449**
Their patience exhausted, launched a fierce attack
On Normandy – to win their territory back.

The French advance was rapid and complete.
Our army collapsed in utter defeat.
And, to add insult to this injury,
By the summer of 1453   **1453**
We'd also lost all our territory
In the south-west, including Gascony.
This represented the worst loss of all:
Ours for three hundred years, Gascony's fall

Meant that, after a century of war,
We 'owned' less of France than ever before.
Just one town remained in English hands: Calais;
And that, of course, was a mere day-trip away.

Domestic affairs

The King was still aged only thirty-two.
Things had been going pretty badly, too,
On the domestic front. His government
Came under pressure, having overspent
Badly on the war. His uncle Humphrey,
Duke of Gloucester, had helped rule the country
Shrewdly during Henry's minority.
A figure of high seniority
In the House of Lancaster, he advised
Wisely and well, so few men were surprised
When his young nephew, as he came of age,
Kept Gloucester in place, rather than engage
Directly in affairs of state himself.
Deeply religious, he applied his wealth
To great centres of learning and knowledge,
Such as King's, Cambridge, and Eton College.

Henry, high-minded and educated,
Was innocent and naïve. He hated
Conflict, confrontation – the very stuff
Of government when the going gets tough.
In 1447 Gloucester died.
The King all but committed suicide
By promoting the widely detested
Duke of Suffolk in his place. Untested,
Dishonest and corrupt, he was impeached
By Parliament when stalemate was reached
In peace talks with France (and other matters).
Fleeing abroad, his career in tatters,
He was murdered by sailors on board ship.
I have to say, "Good riddance, your Lordship!"

Suffolk was succeeded by Somerset
In 1450. The worst crisis yet
In Henry's stormy reign was set to break.
The King made another major mistake
In Somerset. Maladministration
And corruption were crippling the nation.
Heavy taxation and rising prices
Only served to fuel the growing crisis.

Revolt and rebellion

Jack Cade's rebellion was an assault
On the heart of government. His revolt,
With other oppressed smallholders from Kent,
Arose from a deep-seated discontent
With the 'system'. In his manifesto,
He listed which ministers had to go.
Cade's rebels routed a large royal force
At Sevenoaks, then sought to reinforce
Their advantage by marching on London,
Where, to the delight of everyone,
They executed the despised James Fiennes,
The Lord Treasurer. There were early signs,
Though, that Cade lacked vision. A firebrand,
He had no strategy and, poorly-planned,
The insurrection quickly fizzled out.
But of one thing there could be little doubt:
England had teetered, as never before,
On the brink of an all-out civil war.

Henry, moreover, was shocked to the core
By Cade's open identification
With his arch rival (and close relation),
Richard, Duke of York. Dick's family tree
Clearly showed that he just happened to be
Heir to the Earl of March, who, you'll recall,
Was one candidate, after his downfall,

Rhyming History

To succeed poor King Richard the Second.
Bolingbroke seized the crown, though some reckoned
That March, a minor, had the better claim.
It was argued that York, in all but name,
Was now true monarch by rightful descent:
So asserted Cade and the men of Kent.
The Duke, quite wisely, kept a low profile,
Biding his time in self-imposed exile.

But Richard's star was in the ascendant.
Henry had been far too long dependent
On the now discredited Somerset.
He badly needed York's support, and yet
The Duke posed a real and permanent threat.
Childless, Henry knew that his royal line
Would die out with him. That might suit York fine,
But, at the tender age of thirty-two,
Henry felt he still had a lot to do.

Nevertheless, demoralised and tired,
The King was 'on the edge'. Events conspired
To tip him over. Cade's insurrection,
Bankruptcy, chronic lack of direction
In government, woeful losses in France,
Were set-backs hardly likely to enhance
Henry's confidence and sense of self-worth.
Frail, and a martyr to his nerves since birth,
The ailing King, in 1453,
Suffered a collapse, with no guarantee
Of restoration or recovery.
His debilitating insanity
Led to a crisis in the monarchy.

Step forward the Duke of York. It was he,
By virtue of his seniority,
Who became Lord Protector. This could be,
He judged, his perfect opportunity.
Should Henry die, all men would bow the knee

To him, King Richard of the House of York.
He could even help Henry 'take a walk',
If you catch my drift, yet was quite content,
For now, to sit back and see how things went.

Not well, alas! Despite Henry's bad head,
He could still perform, it appeared, in bed.
York's hopes were thwarted by the arrival
Of an heir, securing the survival
Of the royal line. Edward, Prince of Wales,
Of the House of Lancaster, tipped the scales
Once more in Henry's favour. His wee son
Was fragile, but the damage had been done.

The Wars of the Roses

Richard's hopes of an easy transition
Were dashed. He held on to his position
Of Lord Protector for a few more years,
But Queen Margaret resented him. Fears
Of a Yorkist plot tormented the Queen,
Who despised the Duke. She vented her spleen
By recalling the Duke of Somerset.
Richard was livid, and the stage was set
For the Wars of the Roses. The first spat
Occurred at St. Albans. The outcome of that   **1455**
Was the death of Somerset. Lancaster: nil;
York: one. Nothing decisive happened until
1460. The Yorkists captured the King   **1460**
At Northampton, and this changed everything.
The Lancastrians were trounced. It was agreed
That, after Henry's death, Richard should succeed.
So, Henry stayed as King despite his defeat,
But his heirs were disinherited. Quite neat
From Richard's point of view, who, one can surmise,
Anticipated Henry's imminent demise.

Less good from Prince Edward's standpoint, however;
And his mother, Queen Margaret, would never
(I repeat, never) accept such an insult.
So, the fighting continued, with the result
That Richard was slain in battle at Wakefield.
The Yorkists' fate was then apparently sealed
When Henry, early in 1461,   **1461**
Was recaptured by his own side. But York's son,
Another Edward, had his eye on the crown.
The Lancastrians, in a major showdown
At Mortimer's Cross, and then at Towton Moor,
Suffered heavy losses. The King, furthermore,
Weak and exhausted, had lost his appetite
For power. Queen Margaret kept up the fight,
If only on behalf of their son and heir,
Edward, Prince of Wales – but Henry didn't care.

EDWARD THE FOURTH (1461 – 1470; 1471 – 1483)

The family fled to Scotland. There they stayed,
Demoralised, and not a little dismayed
By news of Edward of York's coronation:
Edward the Fourth, Warwick's latest 'creation'.

The Earl of Warwick, nicknamed the 'Kingmaker' –
Although, in the case of Henry, 'King-breaker'
Might be more apposite – had always hated
The King's favourites. He felt underrated,
Insulted, overlooked, humiliated.
Kingmaker Warwick satisfied his grievance
With Henry by transferring his allegiance
To the House of York. King Edward, at nineteen,
Liked drinking and women, and wasn't that keen
On the day-to-day responsibilities
Of kingship. The talents and abilities
Of Warwick served him well. For the first few years,
The Earl ruled the roost. It was sure to end in tears.

Rather like Henry the Fourth's Northumberland,
The ambitious Warwick failed to understand
That the youthful King he'd helped place on the throne
Would want, in due course, to govern on his own.
In 1464, making no pretence   **1464**
At consultation, Edward caused great offence
By marrying a widow of lowly rank,
Elizabeth Woodville. Warwick, to be frank,
Was livid. He had lined up a French princess
For Edward, who, it appeared, couldn't care less
If he offended the surly Earl. The King
Also caused a fuss by negotiating,
Over Warwick's head, a major alliance   **1467**
With Burgundy, this in blatant defiance
Of Warwick's talks with France, Burgundy's sworn foe.

Meanwhile, back to 'King' Henry. At Clitheroe
He was taken captive, for a second time,
In 1465. Henry's only crime

Was failure. A Lancastrian uprising,
The year before, was doomed. It's not surprising,
Given the danger that the former King posed –
He'd not been unequivocally deposed;
He was alive; the Prince of Wales was living;
His tenacious wife was less than forgiving –
That he was confined to the Tower. His son,
However, and the Queen were still on the run.
Edward and Margaret fled to France, from where
They plotted King Edward's death – a lethal pair.

Warwick, in the meantime, was out in the cold.
He opposed a match between Duke Charles the Bold
Of Burgundy and the King's sister. When war   **1468**
With France was mooted, this was the final straw.
The Kingmaker moved swiftly and seized his chance.
In league with Louis the Eleventh of France,
He arrested Edward in a palace *coup.*
He bit off, however, more than he could chew.

The King had established a strong power-base.
Within three months, without undue loss of face,
He regained his freedom. Warwick fled abroad
To France, where he formed an uneasy accord
With Margaret, Henry's disaffected Queen,
And dissident Yorkists. Their collective spleen
They vented by launching a snap invasion   **1470**
Of England, where Edward, on this occasion,
Was surprised and ill-prepared. He in turn fled,
With a few friends, to Burgundy. In his stead,
Henry the Sixth was restored – 're-adepted'
Is the legal term. The poor chap accepted
His fate with patience and equanimity.
He had little choice, though (between you and me)
He was sick to death of the trouble and strife
Whipped up by Queen Margaret, his dreadful wife.

But with Edward the Fourth still at liberty,
Henry's position was very weak. You see,
Nobody knew exactly who the King was!
The majority favoured Edward because,
Quite simply, he'd always looked like a winner,
Whereas Henry made a right old dog's dinner
Of every opportunity he had.
You could almost hear Henry the Fifth, his dad,
Turning in his grave. Edward's exile was short.
He rallied, regrouped and, with valued support
From his brother, Gloucester (of whom more in due course:
You remember the one: "My kingdom for a horse!"),
He returned early in 1471.   **1471**
In April, at Barnet, he fought Warwick and won.

The end of Henry

The Kingmaker fell. Hurrah! The very same day,
Queen Margaret, who'd apparently been away
In France on some kind of extended holiday,
Set sail for England. Lancastrian support
Was strong in Wales, or so her advisers thought.
She landed in Dorset. Her army marched north.
It was a race against time. On May the fourth,
Edward overtook her and, at Tewkesbury,
Scored a sensational, crushing victory.
The Prince of Wales, Henry's heir, died in the field
And even mad Margaret was forced to yield.
The House of Lancaster was hit hard that day,
Its leaders hacked to death, or taken away
To bloody execution. In the Tower
Henry trembled. The hero of the hour,
Edward, had hitherto been too forgiving,
And both men knew it. With Henry still living,
Edward would never be safe – so Henry died.
On the same night as the King's triumphal ride
Through London, Henry breathed his last. Suicide?
Murder? Old age? I shall leave you to decide.

There followed twelve years of comparative calm.
Edward tired of civil strife, and applied balm
To England's deep and festering wounds. At first,
However, he displayed an ill-advised thirst
For war with France. He prepared an invasion.
Parliament needed little persuasion,
Providing him, in 1474,   **1474**
With generous grants – so he went to war.

Perhaps he hankered after the glory days
Of Henry the Fifth, who, in so many ways,
Still stood as the high watermark of success
In matters military. Nevertheless,
Times had changed. Burgundy, Edward's main ally,
Was fickle and poorly-equipped, and fought shy
Of giving practical support. Moreover,
Despite the fact that Edward sailed from Dover
With the largest force in British history,
The French proved formidable, and victory
Eluded our rash King. Luckily for him,
Louis the Eleventh went out on a limb
And offered to buy him out. Parliament   **1475**
Sanctioned his acceptance of a down payment
Of 75,000 gold crowns (goodness!) –
Then two-thirds of that *per annum.* I confess,
I take my hat off to Louis. Cowardice
Was the charge levied at the time. Cleverness,
I call it. Years of bloodshed, pain and distress
Were side-stepped by this rare display of finesse.

So, Edward withdrew his forces. The income,
However craven it may have seemed to some,
Freed him at a stroke from undue dependence
On grants from Parliament. This made good sense.
The King traded with considerable success
On his own account, and in his own ships, no less.
Commerce flourished in the latter years of his reign,
As Edward's subjects were encouraged, once again,

To engage in the business of foreign trade.
With peace, the nation prospered. Fortunes were made,
Not least by the King himself, whose enormous wealth
Was bequeathed to his successors. Chronic ill-health
Dogged the poor fellow and, in 1483,   **1483**
Aged fifty, he died. It's said that debauchery
And sexual excesses were top of the list
Of likely causes. That was the general gist.
I offer no comment. Edward was greatly missed.

Edward's legacy

His progressive reign saw a real improvement
In judicial affairs and law enforcement.
St. George's Chapel, Windsor, was rebuilt –
A nod to God, perhaps, to ease his guilt
Over his saintly predecessor's fate.
A bibliophile, it's hard to overstate
The King's influence. When printing set the trend,
He was there in support, Caxton's patron and friend.

A monarch of passion and imagination,
Edward the Fourth broke the cycle of stagnation,
Bred of civil wars and foreign confrontation,
That kept a stranglehold on the English nation.

RICHARD THE THIRD (1483 – 1485)

Strangleholds, though, were the speciality
Of Edward's wicked successor, Dickie Three.
The whole issue is fraught with controversy,
But Richard the Third, a man without mercy,
Conscience or scruples, was a downright despot,
A murderous tyrant and a thoroughly bad lot.

Edward the Fourth had left two little ones,
Edward and Richard, his surviving sons.

103

Rhyming History

When their father died, Edward succeeded:
King Edward the Fifth. England then needed
A Lord Protector. Enter Uncle Dick.
Richard of Gloucester was clever and quick.
Edward was twelve, and his minority
Wouldn't last long. Richard's priority
Was, first, to ensure his own survival,
Then to clear the field of any rival.
Lord Hastings, loyal brother to the Queen,
Was swiftly executed. More obscene
Was Richard's cleverly argued contention
That his nephews were bastards. Pure invention,
But the Lords and Commons, believe it or not,
Swallowed (hook, line and sinker) Dickie's vile plot.

The Lord Protector announced the postponement
Of Edward's coronation. His enthronement
Never took place. He was sent to the Tower,
And his uncle crowned King within the hour.
'Prince' Edward subsequently 'disappeared',
Along with his kid brother. Few folk cheered
At King Richard's coronation. Foul play
Was suspected. His support ebbed away.
The Princes' bodies were never recovered,
Though two little skeletons were discovered,
In the Tower, in 1674 –
Strongly suggesting that *someone* broke the law.

Richard of Gloucester was only thirty
When he was crowned. Fond of playing dirty,
Some say he may have been responsible –
Hard to prove, but it's not impossible –
For Henry the Sixth's murder in the Tower.
Richard would stop at nothing to seize power,
But this was no way to win friends. His allies
Deserted him, as they came to realise
That, despite his undoubted ability,
He could never deliver the stability

His war-weary subjects so desperately craved.
If Richard hadn't been quite so badly behaved
(That's a euphemism), he might well have survived.

The Battle of Bosworth Field

But war-fever in the kingdom quickly revived
With the landing, in 1485, from France,   **1485**
Of Henry Tudor, with a small force. At first glance,
Henry's prospects were grim. His claim was tenuous,
To say the very least, and Richard strenuous
In defence of his crown. They met at Bosworth Field.
Heavily outnumbered, Henry refused to yield.
Brave and defiant, he fought on the side of right,
While Richard's supporters were too ashamed to fight.
England was exhausted, her new King bankrupt,
The old Yorkist line was broken and corrupt.

The treacherous tyrant met his end that day,
Fighting for his life. There was no other way.
He lived by bloodshed, murder and deceit –
So died he in dishonour and defeat.

Bibliography

Frank Barlow, *The Feudal Kingdom of England, 1042-1216* (Longman, 5th ed. 1999)

John Blair, *The Anglo-Saxon Period* (in *The Oxford History of Britain*, ed. Kenneth O. Morgan – Oxford University Press, 2001)

Peter Hunter Blair, *An Introduction to Anglo-Saxon England* (Cambridge University Press, 2003)

James Campbell (ed.), *The Anglo-Saxons* (Penguin, 1991)

Encyclopaedia Britannica (2010)

Robin Frame, *The Political Development of the British Isles, 1100-1400* (Oxford, 1990)

Sheppard Frere, *Britannia: A History of Roman Britain* (London, 3rd ed. 1987)

John Gillingham, *The Early Middle Ages* (in *The Oxford History of Britain*, ed. Kenneth O. Morgan – Oxford University Press, 2001)

Ralph A. Griffiths, *The Later Middle Ages* (in *The Oxford History of Britain*, ed. Kenneth O. Morgan – Oxford University Press, 2001)

Alan Harding, *England in the Thirteenth Century* (Cambridge University Press, 1993)

F. M. Stenton, *Anglo-Saxon England* (Oxford University Press, 3rd ed. 1971)

G. M. Trevelyan, *A Shortened History of England* (Penguin, 1959)